RETIREMENT
20/20

Winning Retirement Planning for the New Millennium

JEFF CIRINO
CFP®, EA®, CHFC, CLU
Alpha Planning | Solon, Ohio

Jeff Cirino/Alpha Planning
Headquarters
6325 Cochran Road, Suite 5
Solon, OH 44139

Independence Office
4807 Rockside Road, Suite 400
Independence, OH 44131

440.519.0300
https://alphaplanners.com

Retirement 20/20/ Jeff Cirino. —1st ed.

ISBN 978-1689180054

To my generous and loving Elizabeth.

Contents

Introduction i

Chapter 1: Five Questions You Should Ask Any Advisor 1

   *THE FIVE QUESTIONS YOU SHOULD ASK ANY FINANCIAL
ADVISOR* 2

Chapter 2: Hyper-Active Mutual Funds 11

   WHAT IS PHANTOM INCOME TAX? 13

   REAL LIFE EXAMPLE 16

Chapter 3: Tax Collateral Damage 21

   BUCKET #1: TAXABLE IN CURRENT TAX YEAR 21

   *BUCKET #2: TAX-DEFERRED—100% TAXABLE WHEN
DISTRIBUTED* 22

   BUCKET #3: TAX-FREE WHEN DISTRIBUTED 22

   TAX BUCKET #1 23

   TAX BUCKET #2 25

   TAX BUCKET #3 26

   SOME CONCLUDING THOUGHTS ON TAXATION 28

Chapter 4: Mutual Fund and Variable Annuity Costs, Fees,
Charges, and Turnover 29

   MUTUAL FUNDS 29

   *BY THE WAY . . . OWNERS OF MUTUAL FUNDS GET CAUGHT IN
TWO TRAPS* 32

   *VARIABLE ANNUITIES (NOT TO BE CONFUSED WITH FIXED OR
INDEXED ANNUITIES)* 33

Chapter 5: Dividend-Paying Stocks and DRIPS 37

   *DIVIDENDS CAN COME IN THE FORM OF CASH OR SHARES OF
STOCK* 37

   DIVIDEND-PAYING STOCKS 38

   DOW JONES INDUSTRIAL AVERAGE 40

PREFERRED STOCK..*43*

DIVIDEND REINVESTMENT PLAN (DRIPS).............................*45*

PROPER DIVERSIFICATION *46*

Chapter 6: The Principles of Risk and Your Retirement 49

PRINCIPLE 1...*50*

PRINCIPLE 2...*52*

PRINCIPLE 3...*53*

PRINCIPLE 4...*55*

PRINCIPLE 5...*56*

PRINCIPLE 6...*58*

CONCLUSION..*59*

Chapter 7: Exchange-Traded Funds (ETFs) and Indexing...63

Chapter 8: Annuities...71

VARIABLE ANNUITIES *77*

LIFETIME INCOME RIDERS AND INCOME PAYOUT OPTIONS .*81*

A FINAL WORD ABOUT ANNUITIES *82*

Chapter 9: Finding the Right Advisor 83

HOW TO BE CERTAIN YOU FIND AND HIRE THE BEST ADVISOR FOR YOUR UNIQUE FINANCIAL SITUATION *83*

FINAL THOUGHTS...*87*

About the Author..91

Contact Us...93

INTRODUCTION

For more than a decade and counting, I've been a practicing financial planner for people who are fifty years of age and older. I spend my days helping pre- and post-retirees preserve and grow their assets, which in turn provide consistent income for their lifetimes.

The challenges facing both financial advisors and pre- and post-retirees are many. Endless voices compete for your attention every day. A continuous bombardment of "do this," "don't do that," or "buy gold," comes at us 24/7 from radio, TV, mail campaigns, free dinner seminars, and so on. Who should you listen to? That's the first problem people face when attempting to gain 20/20 clarity regarding retirement planning.

10,000 Hours to Reach Expert Level

Many say that to become a master, it takes at least 10,000 hours of practice.[1] That's about 1,000 hours per year for ten years.

I would never presume to know the first thing about what someone else does for a living. And when trying to speak with someone else about their specialty in life, I probably sound kind of dumb to that person. Even if I have some rudimentary knowledge, I can still get confused easily compared to an expert in any complex discussion. So, here's my question to you, the reader: Why would you accept any learning curve on your part when it comes to your own financial survival? This is a particularly relevant question if professional help is out there and available to you.

But it's not always that simple. You need to learn which type of advisors offer independent opinions and develop full-fledged retirement income plans. I want to be clear that I have teachers, engineers, doctors, and scientists as clients—they are all smart, competent professionals in their own areas, and spend plenty of time getting to understand what financial tools and strategies we will use in their plans before we put them in place. They come to me not because I'm some kind of genius (I'm not) or because finance is some unknowable mystery (it's not), but because I've spent decades learning and practicing the fundamentals of planning for retirement. At our firm, we craft comprehensive retirement income plans every day. We've seen what works and

---

[1] Jordan Scheltgen. Inc.com. January 9, 2018. "It Takes 10,000 Hours to Become an Expert in Anything: Use These 4 Techniques." https://www.inc.com/jordan-scheltgen/it-takes-10000-hours-to-become-an-expert-in-anything-use-these-4-techniques.html

what doesn't. We have enough experience to know some strategies are superior to others. But a client does not often get the chance to see firsthand how these concepts work until they are actually putting their own plan into action. They haven't had numerous fly-on-the-wall experiences or seen how one particular strategy performs over time compared to another. Because they haven't lived as a financial planner, they don't automatically understand all detailed aspects of a plan or spot high-level issues at a glance.

To this date, I have personally logged well more than 25,000 hours in this field. I can tell you there is no learning curve for us except learning about you and your wishes in retirement.

While going it alone may be tempting, any mistakes a person makes in planning for retirement could come with a serious price tag. I find prudent people do not want to experiment with the future of their nest egg. It's not easy for people to know where to turn for help. Why? Largely because only a handful of financial advisors actually take the time, up front, to hammer out comprehensive retirement plans. This is the core of preparing for retirement, and the client and advisor should plan for that before they cement any kind of relationship. By a comprehensive plan, I mean a maximum integration that accounts for but is not limited to Social Security, pensions, assets, income, inflation, and taxes. All these elements must be combined into one master plan, which should then be updated each year. At our practice, Alpha Planning, we believe this planning should ideally occur over several meetings (three to six) to allow clients to become comfortable with new concepts. Then they can judge how they feel about our findings or recommendations. This allows for the

20/20 clarity we want clients to gain so their plans can be properly implemented.

A pure, sales-type broker or advisor is the very last thing you need at this critical point in your life.

As an advisor, I have reviewed literally hundreds of portfolios. After years of evaluation, I am now an expert at detecting one primary destructive pattern. Can you guess what that pattern is? That's right: advisors who put product sales before any due process of careful planning. For instance, some work with fifty-and-overs, but have zero Social Security knowledge. As someone who considers every aspect of a client's portfolio, the practice of eliminating Social Security from the retirement picture is ludicrous.

For those closing in on retirement, I hope you give this book a close read. I hope it reaches you at any stage of pre- or post-retirement. I hope to dispel some of the myths and misconceptions people hold about money that often keep them from making the wisest financial decisions. The truths uncovered in this book stare right into the face of the many falsehoods and smokescreens created by both the media and the financial industry itself.

Americans suffer from a continuous state of doubt and fear, as well as remorse regarding any bad decisions they may have made in the past. To make matters worse, ads and commercials endlessly bombard us. Propaganda like this wants us to second-guess past and future decisions. They motivate us to desire what they promote, even if it is unnecessary or even harmful.

Fear sells. But the clarity of a good advising team will help you live without fear or regret.

In this book, we will discuss how to recognize and reduce many of the unnecessary fees, costs, and taxes that are causing your retirement dollars to fall through the cracks in your portfolio.

One significant and undeniable result of the Great Recession is that people grew more cognizant of costs and risks that *can* and *do* rob them of much of their savings. Indeed, people today live with more awareness of the concept of risk. They want to know how much risk they are really taking.

Risk downside increases in magnitude for those who are older than fifty. Many now realize the inevitable great drawdowns from market corrections can be recovered only so many times during one's lifetime.

Everyone is in business to make a living. Most people would agree with that. Within the financial industry, some wish to act as stewards, while others are just in it for themselves.

From my personal experience reviewing hundreds of portfolios, I can honestly say at least 80 percent of people are paying 1 to 3 percent *more* each year than is necessary on their investments. This has quite the negative exponential effect, which becomes staggering over time. Additionally, they receive insufficient tax advice that can be very damaging, resulting in another erosions of their savings.

Tax planning is probably the most overlooked part of retirement plans. Tax losses shorten the lifespan of your money. Tax losses are worse than market losses. In the case of market losses, if you hold, those account values will—eventually—come back. But tax losses due to ignorance means your money disappears, never to return, making it a true lost opportunity.

In the following chapters, I will take you through the journey and process that many advisors, myself included, developed over the years with *real* people in the *real* world. One thing we all know about life is that change is a constant. The planning process is a living, breathing thing and should be viewed as an evolving process. In short, planning should be done first, but your plan's success also requires year-by-year updates, monitoring, and tracking.

I thank you in advance for investing your valuable time to educate yourself and for giving me the honor of your attention. I hope to give you a 20/20 look behind the curtain of the retail financial services world. Hidden things are hidden for a reason . . . and it's never good.

Chapter 1

FIVE QUESTIONS YOU SHOULD ASK ANY ADVISOR

Life is 10 percent what happens to you
and 90 percent how you respond to it.
~ Charles R. Swindoll

Everyone is different. Be thankful that's the case, because it would be a very boring life if we weren't. These differences challenge advisors to be flexible with each client while tethered to bellwether planning concepts.

The biases people have when they first visit a new advisor can play a big part in whether they can grasp or be comfortable with new concepts. It can also mean the difference between the success and failure of your savings' ability to work throughout your retirement.

Now, when considering a financial advisor, you should consider asking these few high-level questions. Among them:

• How do you get paid?
• How good is your website?
• How many years have you been in business?

Yet these basic questions, among others, represent the tip of the iceberg of questions you need to ask any advisor.

What do you ask an advisor when you don't know what you don't know?

People often don't even know what questions to ask an advisor when making important financial decisions. I'll give you the inside scoop here: Most people I meet with don't know what to ask. But, when I'm helping clients or friends vet other professionals in the industry, I have five questions that cover most of what I think actually matters. This is what I use as a filter, and you can, too. If someone you're considering for your financial advisor can't give satisfactory answers to these five questions, then you most likely need to move on down the list.

THE FIVE QUESTIONS YOU SHOULD ASK ANY FINANCIAL ADVISOR

Question One: Have you adequately reviewed my personal financial situation to make sure this recommendation is in my best interest?

This sounds simple. But think about it this way: it should take an advisor *at least* two meetings to gather the necessary information to develop an appropriate analysis of your current situation. If a financial advisor has not taken time to probe into your current situation before he or she presents a working financial plan, you will inevitably discover that the plan you are being shown is less than custom, including potentially devastating shortcuts. Unfortunately, sometimes in this business, financial professionals submit recommendations to clients before enough upfront data gathering or strategizing takes place. Obviously, these shortcuts occur more often with product salespeople than with "planning" advisors.

Far too often, only a cursory gathering of information takes place, making it impossible for the advisor to develop a comprehensive financial plan.

These early steps are so important that the CERTIFIED FINANCIAL PLANNER™ Board of Standards recommends the very first steps in the financial planning process are to gather information on the *current* circumstances, and to define the scope of the advisor/client engagement. While an advisor and their office gather a person's current data, they should simultaneously develop the scope of the current assets, living situation, and potential, along with the client's goals or targets. This involves the client's specific goals or intentions, plus any other time-sensitive issues he or she is facing.

Question Two: How will your plan affect my tax return each year and what future tax issues may concern me?

When you were young and saving toward the future, you did not need in-depth tax planning. At that point in your life, your goals could be summed up by one word: growth. When you retire, financial strategies become 100 percent inverted.

If you are older than fifty, you should now be in the distribution phase of the financial cycle. The distribution phase still includes a growth component, but you cannot look at this one-dimensionally. At this stage, your finances are a combination of distributions, tax management, safety, and a little growth. It's no longer just growth, growth, growth.

Tax planning is a critical component in a complete financial plan that preserves and extends the life of your money. Most large financial firms expressly prohibit any tax information coming from their sales force. Mostly, this is because they don't want any liability. And, to be clear, a financial advisor is not the same as a tax professional. Yet, planning for retirement in a vacuum and putting taxes out of mind until April is incredibly foolhardy. By then, the tax horse is already out of the proverbial barn door.

Why you should be concerned about taxes.

First and foremost, tax losses are worse than market losses.

Why? Value lost in a market account may not be lost forever—as long as you aren't taking withdrawals from the account while it's down, there is a good chance a losing account could pop back up at a later time. When you lose money through taxes, they disappear forever. Tax losses are purely a lost opportunity cost, plain and simple. But do not despair! Taxes are also something you can control to a great extent if you're working alongside a knowledgeable advisory team.

In the tax planning chapter, I will share with you many unknowns and explain the critical bond between retirement planning and tax planning.

Many advisors give advice from a pure accumulation and investment standpoint, but they fail to take into consideration the annual or future tax erosion of that investment. Many people fear market risk and are alarmed at the very thought of losing money in the market. However, a financial strategy with unknown tax results can give rise to greater collective losses than one bad year in the market.

There are many pitfalls created from inefficient tax investments and unwise account withdrawals. It takes a well-trained and experienced financial advisor to prevent this. A good advisor can help you implement strategies that take into account short- and long-term benefits from all standpoints related to tax planning.

All too often, people focus on the wrong things and ignore tax implications. But I urge you to evaluate both with equal importance. I cannot over-emphasize the magnitude of this point. If your financial advisor has not even looked at your tax return, you need to ask, "Why?" Depending on the answer, you might need to find another advisor.

Question Three: How will your plan affect my income as well as my liquidity needs in the future?

Unfortunately, many plans or products that are "sold" to people fail to account for details such as liquid emergency funds. This may be because, often, liquid funds mean funds an advisor isn't directly benefitting from because the client by definition keeps them off to the side, separate from their investment and income plans. The advisor doesn't profit from money you keep at the bank. Yet, appropriate liquidity is incredibly important to the overall success of a plan. You will need enough to cover an emergency or unexpected situation.

It's an important note that many seniors greatly overestimate the amounts needed for emergencies. Too much money sitting around in an account with little return for many years adds up to ongoing lost opportunity costs. This overemphasis can be prevented by having a detailed financial plan that accounts for every aspect of your retirement finances. That way, you aren't just guessing at your liquidity needs. A plan can really be liberating and empowering because it gives you visible, tangible results. Confidence based only on reality is the name of the game. Once again, if you don't get an adequate answer about how a professional handles the liquidity piece of your financial picture, you will want to consider moving to another advisor.

Question Four: How does your plan match up with my risk comfort level?

Financial advisors have always asked this question regarding risk. Yet, historically many investors have taken more risk than they realize, only understanding the full scope of their risks when a market downturn occurs. The majority of financial advisors may refer to risk as a catchword when visiting with clients. Sadly, they still concentrate on potential returns based almost entirely on an investment's history. But what's that disclaimer on the bottom of anything market-facing? "Past performance does not indicate future results." In other words, past performance in the investment field means next to nothing. Shoddy SEC regulations on mutual fund transparency underscore this problem. I will dig deeper into what I mean about this in the remainder of the book, but suffice it to say the public isn't even looking closely at the real past returns when evaluating many of the most popular investing products.

RISK = The only time you'll call your advisor's actions or advice into question is when your account is going down. Have you ever heard of someone calling their advisor when an account is sharply up 9 percent to thank them for doing such a great job? Do not focus only on high returns. There is always an inverted reality, or whipsaw, that goes along with high risk.

It is an easily observed phenomena that people react more emotionally when things are down than when things are up. From social media to the constant news cycle, it's the negative we often react to. One result of the "Great Recession" of 2008 is people were seriously looking eye-to-eye at the consequences of high risk. Prior to the first decade of this century, people were getting 1990s fever. In the '90s, the populace became intoxicated by the potential rates of return on their investments, which were virtually unsustainable. Investors today have actually seen losses firsthand and more recently in their own accounts. This also happens in the accounts of people who are just about to retire. They see how those losses drastically and permanently affect their ability to obtain the highest income going forward. Risk assessment contributes in huge ways to prudent financial planning.

The mid-2010s saw a strong bull market, tempting many to fall back asleep and neglect risk management. This looks very similar to the times when the industry rode the roller coaster up, only to ride it back down—like pre-2008 all over again. You may also remember how the hubbub of 2008 led Congress and other institutions with financial oversight to tighten up many regulations and change standards for the betterment of investment practices. However, very quietly, the industry crept back in with risky credit rules for institutions. Risky credit rules were the cause of the whole mess in the first place. The Trump administration has reversed nearly all safeguards that were put into place for investors after the meltdown.

From my standpoint, now more than ever, it is imperative that your financial professional be on the same page with you when it comes to the question of risk and how to handle it.

Question Five: How will your plan affect the transition of my estate to my heirs?

Legacy is in question here. First though, an advisor should take care to make sure their clients will not outlive their money. I have yet to meet the person whose fondest dream is to ask their children for money, or whose Plan A is living in their kids' basement. Rather, many people think the greatest gift they can give their children and themselves is to never *have* to live with them if they do not want to. The second objective an advisor should have, however, is to ensure the responsible transfer of wealth—which can have various meanings to be sure. This certainly looks different for different people—priorities, family relationships, various circumstances all determine what this actually means. The overarching point here is you will want to make sure the value of your estate will go to your designated beneficiaries and not to the government or probate lawyers. While some of this is up to actions you take with an estate planning attorney, your financial advisor is crucial to this success. A financial professional who isn't knowledgeable about legacy planning strategies and who isn't prepared to help you and your estate planner execute various strategies is probably not the professional you should work with in retirement.

So, there you have it: The five critical questions you should ask any financial advisor. Just these five questions alone have now made you more empowered than 90 percent of your peers. You should use these queries to develop your self-confidence when dealing with your current or any future advisors. After all, the main purpose of this book is to help people regain ownership of their money.

You shouldn't rush the financial planning process. When you are looking for the right financial advisor, take whatever time is necessary, ask the five questions, and do a thorough look forward in terms of review and analysis.

Take control of your finances by following the process I have outlined in the chapters of this book. It is time for you to reclaim ownership of your retirement. Your future depends on it!

Chapter 2
HYPER-ACTIVE MUTUAL FUNDS
& PHANTOM INCOME TAX ON NON-IRAS

The hardest thing in the world to understand is the income tax.
~Albert Einstein

B efore understanding phantom income tax, it's important to have a basic understanding of *mutual funds*. You might be familiar with the term "mutual fund" but not understand how these financial tools actually operate.

The Investment Company Act of 1940 first created the mutual fund, and now the Securities and Exchange Commission (or SEC) regulates them. You're likely well acquainted with the idea of a stock, where you are purchasing an individual share of ownership in a company. A mutual fund is a pool of several companies' stocks.

Some of the most commonly known investment companies include Fidelity, Vanguard, and Putnam. Each investment company manages the accounts at their will within the objectives of the fund's charter, stated in the prospectus. Every mutual fund shareholder receives a prospectus, but few can make it through all the jargon to understand the plain-language objectives of their mutual fund.

Mutual funds can also contain additional securities such as bonds, money market instruments, corporate notes, government bonds, and even alternative assets.

Each shareholder of a mutual fund participates proportionally in the gain or loss of the fund. Each shareholder also shares in the "phantom income tax" liability as well.

Active or Hyperactive Funds

This is the kind of mutual fund most people still have due to pressure from sales outlets, especially the big box advisory firms. These funds are actively traded daily, triggering costs deducted from the fund's value. These funds are the primary culprit of phantom income tax and hidden turnover expenses.

I'm convinced 99 percent of the public will never receive a plain-English explanation of what fund turnover is and how it hurts returns by triggering phantom income tax. It is interesting that investors are seldom shown these characteristics by advisors *before* they're told to put their money into such funds.

Passive Funds

These are indexed funds and exchange-traded funds. Even though they are called passive, they are watched and rebalanced periodically. The advantages of a passive fund are industry-low expenses and less trading, which means fewer turnover costs.

WHAT IS PHANTOM INCOME TAX?

I have found it to be interesting and eye-opening to ask people attending our workshops if they have ever heard of phantom income tax. Rarely do I see a hand go up.

I then ask if there's anyone in the room who experienced a fund going down in value in a year, but then end up receiving a capital gains tax bill in the mail? Several heads always nod at that. In a nutshell, this is the reality of phantom taxation.

Take a second here to digest . . . what I just described is tax due on money you were never able to spend in the first place. This is equivalent to getting kicked in the head after someone runs you over with their car. It does not have to be this way. Plenty of leaner and meaner investments exist out there. They are just not presented to the public by "commission-based" advisors.

It bears repeating. Your mutual fund loses money in a given year, and then you are taxed on gains that never truly existed. You weren't able to use these gains at any time. Instead, you have to write a check to the IRS for "gains" after a year of flat or even down performance.

Mutual funds do not pay federal income taxes on the funds bought and sold within the fund. But somebody has to. And guess who it is?

Gains on non-IRA mutual funds are passed on to the shareholders. Sadly, this occurs even when your overall account is flat or down on the year. Phantom income tax occurs when more winners than losers are *realized* (made real and taxable) in a year by the fund itself.

According to *The Trouble with Mutual Funds*, by Richard Rutner, a couple of little-known rules not only stilt a fund's growth potential, but also serve as another trigger for phantom income tax.

• The 5 Percent Rule: No fund can have more than 5 percent of any stock. So, when winners really start to expand, the fund is forced to sell enough to get back under the 5 percent rule. The stock is sold reluctantly by the fund because the stock's performance made it take up more of the value of a fund than was allowed. Did you know that?

• The Liquidity Problem: When investors flee from a fund and demand redemptions, the fund must liquidate whatever is necessary to turn the request to cash in seven days or less. Once again, this causes underperformance, dilutes returns, and triggers phantom income tax. Did you know this? Also, when markets collapse, people unwisely flee and cash in their funds. So, the manager must sell, sell, sell into a declining market.

Allow me to elaborate a bit more. For example, individual stocks within a mutual fund will fluctuate daily. Some days they will be up in price and some days they will be down. But their fate isn't to be "winners" or "losers" until they are sold. That is when a "realized gain" or a "realized loss" takes place. It is very possible for a fund manager to sell off stock for a gain, but still have the mutual fund overall lose money over the course of a year. If a portion of the mutual fund is sold for a gain, the investor then becomes responsible for the taxation on that capital gain, even if the value on your statement is less than it was at the beginning of the year.

Until the fund manager actually sells the losers, they cannot be used to offset the winners that were "realized" within the fund. So, the difference is not just how many winners and losers there are over a year, but how many winners and losers have been "realized," or sold.

Keep in mind, the fund manager's job is to maximize the portfolio for maximum return, and they will try to show more winners than losers. Having a clear understanding of "realized" gains and losses versus "unrealized" gains and losses is key. Again, realized gains or losses occur when the fund sells the stock. The portfolio's paper statement may say it lost or gained money, but the realization of that loss or gain is not "real" until it is sold. So, once again, the value of a mutual fund can be down, but it will only be *realized* (or made real to the investor) when it is sold. Phantom income tax is triggered when you have more realized gains than realized losses in a year.

REAL LIFE EXAMPLE

I had a couple come to me with this very problem. They had $350,000 invested in a portfolio of various mutual funds and the account lost about $90,000 in one year: a 27 percent loss. However, they still had a capital gain of about $1,500, which resulted in $225 in taxes at the end of the year. They were clearly victims of phantom income tax. It's very likely someone reading this book has had something very similar happen to them. In this case, the fund went up a lot in the first half of the year. But then it flattened during the second half of the year. The mutual fund manager sold the winners because he wanted to realize wins.

Remember, the mutual fund manager's objective is to make money for the fund, not to do your tax planning. The mutual fund manager is focused on keeping his job by getting the highest returns possible. These folks are under immense pressure to produce winners.

This is not a criticism of fund managers. It is simply an explanation of how mutual funds work, and how it affects your bottom line.

How often can phantom income happen?

It might happen three to four years out of every ten. A classic scenario of a calendar year that triggers phantom income tax is 2013. You often have a strong market in the first four to six months of the calendar year. Then it's either flat or down for the rest of the year. This pattern is just one of many patterns that occur without your control. It's the nature of the active mutual fund beast.

Why does the phantom income tax happen with mutual funds and not stocks or ETFs?

While it is possible, phantom income tax does not frequently happen in exchange-traded funds (or ETFs) or passive funds in part because these funds experience less turnover. It happens in mutual funds more often due to the regulatory construct of active mutual funds versus the tax treatment of stocks or ETF gains. It's really that simple. Tax on money you are not using to live on in any tax year is like keeping your shower on twenty-four hours a day when it's used for less than one hour.

How can you reduce or eliminate phantom income tax?

If you own mutual funds solely, you cannot control it. The fund is actually in control of your money from a tax standpoint. However, if you have other assets, you can use them to offset some taxes by taking realized losses on some of your other investments. You can entirely eliminate phantom income tax by substituting active mutual funds with stocks or ETFs. By doing this you can exercise more control over when to pay for realizing capital gains.

You're in more control and not at the random mercy of an investment company. In other words, *you* are in control of how and when you are taxed. Not somebody else.

Why is it legal for an advisor to not tell you about the phantom income tax?

First, there is a lack of transparency intrinsic in the very minimal regulations of these funds. Really, it's a tax consequence that comes from what it is.

Second, a commissioned salesperson is not required to tell about the potential of phantom income tax. In fact, many of them are not even aware of phantom income tax themselves. A lack of tax knowledge by the advisor alone is a plausible reason they never bring this subject up with an investor.

Phantom income tax is not anything illegal or unethical. However, it is kicking you and your investments while they are down. It's not the most attractive feature of a mutual fund.

What should your financial advisor do if you have mutual funds invested in a non-IRA?

As a financial advisor, the first thing I would do is look at your tax return. The standard for sound tax planning is to first identify it, then quantify it, and rectify it. By reviewing your tax return, we can see the exact source of any gain because it will be listed in an itemized section of the tax return.

Unfortunately, anything that's already happened cannot be reversed. However, your advisor can make recommendations to help you avoid phantom income tax in the future. A good advisor will always look ahead to determine how to prevent these types of unintended consequences.

What alternative financial instruments can I use to avoid the phantom income tax?

ETFs, individual stocks, and fixed index annuities are all potentially a great antidote for the phantom income tax problem. ETFs often accomplish multiple financial objectives by triggering less taxation, no phantom income tax, and less net expenses than their actively managed mutual fund counterparts. You don't have to have the risk of individual stock. An ETF is only one piece of a diversified portfolio that has possibly hundreds of stocks inside it, so you don't have the intrinsic risk that you do with individual stocks. ETFs are more tax efficient, and if they are used in a proper design, you can achieve a very respectable return on a tax-favored basis at minimal cost.

How can I find out if *my* funds are vulnerable?

If you want to do your own research, you can find resources that will give you information about particular funds that alert you about their tendencies toward a phantom income tax. One of the best resources is the Morningstar® report. Morningstar® is an independent rating service for mutual funds, stocks, and exchange-traded funds. In that report, you would look at the turnover statistics for your mutual fund. The level of turnover will be the "canary in the coal mine" when sniffing for phantom income tax potential. If the turnover percentage is over 50 percent per year, you are beginning to get into the likely phantom income tax and high-expense zone. Many funds have annual turnover ranging from 80 to 150 percent, and even much higher. In global funds, the price spread is greater than domestic funds and 100 percent turnover could cost you an additional 3 percent in fees or taxes per year, or more.

Turnover is when a mutual fund manager at an investment company buys and sells his whole portfolio in a twelve-month period. In other words, if you look at a Morningstar® report and you see that turnover is at 100 percent or higher, which is fairly common, that means the fund manager bought and sold every single position that he started with in the course of the year. If it's 300 percent, it means the fund manager has bought and sold every single position that he started with three times in a year. Along with certain market trends, higher turnover can trigger a lot of phantom income tax. Conversely, any fund with less than a 10 percent turnover rate would generate a very minimal phantom income tax.

Accountants and tax preparers understand the concept of phantom income tax and can explain it. However, it is unlikely they will take the time to offer any advice regarding how to eliminate it. When a tax preparer has hundreds or even thousands of tax returns running through their office in any given year, they have a very limited amount of time they can spare to offer advice for future planning for any individual. They are looking at your tax return more as a historian. There are a number of great tax preparers and CPAs who do forward tax planning, but the majority of them typically do not have the time because their time is consumed with getting a large volume of returns prepared. Phantom income tax can cause a lot of dollars to fall through the cracks in your money. It is just another financial erosion to your investments, and one you can remedy.

Chapter 3

TAX COLLATERAL DAMAGE
IRAS AND REQUIRED MINIMUM DISTRIBUTION (RMD)

*The avoidance of taxes is
the only intellectual pursuit
that carries any reward.
~John Maynard Keynes*

For the purposes of this chapter, I would like you to take a 30,000-foot view of all of your assets. Take the aggregate number of all your retirement accounts and resources. Now divide that number into three buckets:

BUCKET #1: TAXABLE IN CURRENT TAX YEAR

The total of all non-IRA funds you have. These are monies in joint or individual ownership form, but not IRAs, 401(k)s, or Roth IRAs.

BUCKET #2: TAX-DEFERRED—100% TAXABLE WHEN DISTRIBUTED

Here you have all your traditional IRA/401(k)/403(b)/457 plans. Although these investment vehicles have their own rules and particulars, they are taxed the same when distributed (at your highest ordinary income tax rate) and so for the purposes of this chapter, we will refer to all of these tax-qualified accounts simply as "IRAs." Most people have considerably more in this bucket than the other two.

BUCKET #3: TAX-FREE WHEN DISTRIBUTED

In this bucket, you will only have your Roth IRAs and any cash value life insurance policies.

As you may already know, traditional IRAs are tax-deferred until money is withdrawn. This means all growth is deferred until withdrawn.

And when they are withdrawn, they are taxable at the highest ordinary income rates for an individual or couple. Non-IRAs are not tax-deferred by default, but you can position them into tax-deferred status.

However, non-IRAs are taxed only on the gain *above* your principal. Non-IRAs are items like joint accounts, revocable living trust accounts, individual accounts, accounts that transfer on death or are payable on death.

Again, for the sake of the exercise in this chapter, think of your money in terms of the tax qualities of each of the three buckets.

Many advisors and self-investors focus more on the returns, costs, risks, and all the other prudent things one considers when making an investment decision. Those things are *crucial* and *critical* points. However, before an advisor gives you a recommendation, they—and you—need to fully understand the investment's current tax treatment as well as its future tax consequences. Unfortunately, people frequently miss or underestimate tax consequences until it is too late. Not being ahead of future tax issues can have a significantly negative impact on your assets.

You will recall in the previous chapter we covered phantom income tax in non-IRA accounts as a real cost that can reduce your net returns. If you are still unclear about phantom income tax, I suggest you stop here and re-read the previous chapter. In addition to checking a new investment's costs, performance, risk level, and the fund's objectives, you should look at it in an accurate tax context. Unfortunately, many advisors put the cart before the horse when making investment recommendations, which can set the investor up for substantial financial losses.

TAX BUCKET #1

(taxable in current year only)

In Tax Bucket #1, you should only designate current income-generating assets you need to live on and are using to meet your current living expenses. This could be non-IRA money. It could be money you use as an income stream from an IRA, but once you take it out of the IRA, it becomes non-IRA money. This amount will vary from person-to-person and from household-to-household depending on the chosen lifestyle and level of monthly expenses.

As you know, if you are receiving income from an asset, the IRS requires you to pay tax on it by April 15 of the year following the year it was received. For the purposes of this chapter, we are assuming you are not using any sophisticated tax-reduction strategies to offset any taxable income.

So, once again, if you are receiving income in this calendar year, you will be subject to current income tax. Most people do not argue this point.

Unfortunately, many, many investors are paying tax on much more than what they are using for living expenses. Because they have more in Tax Bucket #1 than just their living expense money. They are receiving income, interest, and or dividends on a "tax-disadvantaged" basis (highest ordinary income brackets) when they are not using that money to live on in the current year. What is the result? The result is an annual depletion of your funds by annual tax exposure on the income (you currently aren't using) from assets. Consequently, you have lost the purchasing power of the money lost each year. Also, consider the lost opportunity cost now and in the future.

Line 8a on the IRS 1040 tax return will show the tax-exposed income from interest and ordinary dividends. This income is added to your other earned and investment income for the year and is consequently reduced by taxation, year after year. This is just another way money falls through the cracks for people time and time again.

In summary, you should only have money in Tax Bucket #1 for monies actually used for your expenses in a given year.

TAX BUCKET #2

(100 percent taxable when distributed)

Assets in Tax Bucket #2 should be reserved for income you *may* need on a sporadic basis or if you need to generate an additional income stream at some indefinite time in the future. This bucket is for unscheduled or unplanned lumps. Bucket #2 is best used as an intermediate "war chest" to be used for income to replace pensions or Social Security income lost from the death of a spouse. This bucket could also be used for additional income to supplement other income streams, such as Social Security or pensions. In other words, when inflation starts to noticeably give you less mileage per dollar than it used to, you would use income from the assets in Bucket #2 as you need it. But, until you do need it, it should not be subject to annual taxation like funds in Bucket #1.

Let me give you an analogy I briefly alluded to earlier. You came to my house for dinner one evening, and as we were dining, you heard the shower running upstairs. At that point you may ask, "Is someone upstairs taking a shower?" I would respond, "No. I leave the shower on just in case I may want to take a shower later this evening." You would think I was crazy, and you would be right. You would think I was insane to waste water in such a manner, instead of just turning it on and off only when needed.

If you think wasting water is foolish, then what do you think about people who pay voluntary annual taxation on money they are not currently using? There is absolutely no difference. Waste is waste.

The bottom line is this: If you aren't using the money, don't put it in investment vehicles where it will be subject to your highest current tax rates.

TAX BUCKET #3

(Tax-deferred and tax-free when distributed)

This tax pocket is the last bastion of funds for an individual or couple. In Bucket #3, you should put the money that is a tax-free option for your income. It is not subject to current taxation.

Items in this bucket may be assets such as Roth IRAs and life insurance. This bucket has a zero-tax bracket, and if possible, money from Bucket #2 should be gradually moved over into Bucket #3 by Roth conversions or life insurance for tax-free withdrawals.

How do you know if you have the correct assets in the right buckets?

Your tax return will tell you if you have the correct assets in the correct bucket. If you don't know how to obtain this information from your tax return, find a qualified professional who can help.

How do I stop these tax leaks?

I promised earlier in this chapter to provide you with some examples of how to stop these tax leaks from occurring in income-producing assets you are not currently using. Here are five of the many solutions:

1. As I mentioned in the previous chapter, one of the solutions to stop phantom income tax is to use exchange-traded funds or stocks instead of mutual funds in non-IRA accounts. ETFs have negligible turnover, thus no phantom income tax. ETFs can also receive qualified dividend treatment (lower capital gains rates).

2. Place your tax-exposed funds in a growth portfolio that does not pay dividends. Note, you should only use stocks, ETFs, or structured market portfolios to accomplish this. You should *not* use active mutual funds, or you will find yourself driving around the same tax "cul-de-sac" I have been describing.

3. Shelter money in Bucket #2 in a tax-deferred annuity. If you need unscheduled withdrawals, they are available. Or, if you need to add a permanent income source at some future point, annuities can be a great resource for that, as well.

4. Avoid variable annuities due to their exorbitant and often undisclosed fees, charges, and other costs.

5. You can use a cash-heavy, low-death benefit life insurance policy. From these accounts you can pull out tax-free money up to what you have funded it with. This is a very good tax-favored vehicle to use.

If you are wealthy, or somewhat wealthy, you can donate a highly appreciated business or property, receive tax-free income from a charitable trust, avoid the capital gain on the appreciated asset, and produce tax-free income to your heirs. This is accomplished through charitable remainder trust planning.

To establish this kind of trust planning, only work with advisors who are very qualified in this area. This is a very specialized area and must be done correctly. Not only do you need a financial advisor, you also need an attorney, a trust entity, and a CPA. Realize, however, that it's worth it.

SOME CONCLUDING THOUGHTS ON TAXATION

I hope it has become apparent as to why I wanted you to only think of your assets in terms of taxable and tax-deferred assets. You will want to make sure you are paying taxes only on the money you are using to fund your current lifestyle. More importantly, you should know the difference between the performance of an asset and the taxable treatment of an asset. They are each very distinct and critical for your financial success or failure.

At this point, some of you may still be confused. Don't feel bad. The Internal Revenue Code is very complicated. Without training or the help of a qualified investment advisor or tax advisor, it is easy to become confused.

At a minimum, the takeaway from this chapter and the three tax buckets concept should be that you have choices with how you can structure your investments. You can do so without giving up any investment advantage related to your current income. Armed with this knowledge, you are now more empowered to have more control over how and when you generate taxable income, so you can keep more of your money.

Chapter 4

MUTUAL FUND AND VARIABLE ANNUITY COSTS, FEES, CHARGES, AND TURNOVER

Expenses are what kill investor returns.
The more expenses and people you have
between you and your money, the less you keep.
~Warren Buffet

Variable annuities are NOT the same as fixed indexed annuities. Do not confuse them.

MUTUAL FUNDS

Before discussing the costs, fees, and charges inside mutual funds and variable annuities, let's first look at the big picture of long-term investing.

Myth: Often people think, after staring at the Dow Jones Industrial average, their portfolio should be doing the same as that index. I have observed this phenomenon, and I can assure you it is a fallacy and a myth. There are a few reasons most investments do not mirror the price movements of the Dow; it is incorrect intuitive logic that leads one to think they should in the first place.

First, indexes cannot allow for timing issues when building a portfolio. For indexes, there is no "getting in" and "getting out" of the market. Secondly, the indexes do not have costs associated with them. Costs are like pin holes in a balloon. They have the potential to deflate your financial balloon significantly.

A 2018 Dalbar study vividly illustrates this reality. The study showed the average return for investors over the previous twenty years was only 3.00 percent. Over the previous ten years, it was less than negative one-half of one percent or (-0.50).[2] There are two primary reasons for this outcome. Remember, indices are benchmarks, but there is no reason you should presume your money will follow the indices or even mirror them.

The Dalbar study shows investors often get into an investment at the very worst time (new market highs) and also leave an investment at the very worst time (market lows). There are various reasons for this, but it happens. The second reason is that investors are not cognizant of the *true* costs assessed on their capital (what their investments really cost in total). That's what I've been preaching for the past twenty-five years and that's what this chapter is about.

---

[2] 2018 QAIB Qualitative Analysis of Investor Behavior prepared by Dalbar, Inc. Research & Communications Division March 2018.

Before anyone ever goes into an investment, the first thing they should do is look at a Morningstar® report on the fund or stock they are considering. Many financial professionals will print a report for you for free. If someone is presenting a mutual fund to you, they should show you a Morningstar® report. We can all agree a typical mutual fund prospectus is very long and wordy, and investors do not find them helpful. If your advisor hasn't already, I encourage you to ask them to provide you with a third-party report.

There are four specific places on the report that should catch your attention. First, look at the "front-end load" of the fund. Some funds don't have a front-end load, but many do. A front-end load is an immediate cost you will incur to initially invest in a fund and it is an immediate drain on your short-term potential gain. Loads of any kind put you in the hole on the very day you go into the market and drag on it long-term. For example, if your investment in the fund is $100, your 5.75 percent load makes you buy-in at $105.75. This starts you off at a loss the very first day you purchase a fund. In other words, until the mutual fund's price goes up to $105.75, you are at a loss.

Secondly, you should also look at the 12b-1 fees or annual expense ratios. These fees are derived from the regulatory code that governs. It is simply an annual marketing and advertising fee that is assessed to the fund holders. This expense is primarily so a fund can advertise and get *more* people to invest in the mutual fund. This fee is considered an operational expense and is generally between 0.25 percent and 1 percent, although it can be more, annually.

BY THE WAY . . . OWNERS OF MUTUAL FUNDS GET CAUGHT IN TWO TRAPS

Most funds must stay 80 percent invested at all times. This means when markets periodically dip or even crash, your funds are still sitting in the middle of the market pounding. However, once a person knows what to look for, they usually don't allow that cost to get by them again. These fees are one of the biggest reasons why individual mutual funds will not mirror the indexes.

Once again, when a fund reports performance, they report the gross growth, not growth minus expenses or net returns. In my opinion, we need more regulations for mutual funds that will increase disclosure and transparency for the safety and benefit of the public. The investor should not have to translate the real costs associated with an investment. All the related costs should be explained clearly, so there is no question or even a hint of non-disclosure. Funds—in my opinion—should be required to translate the turnover rate into actual stated costs, as well as the expense ratio and operating expenses. This should be in plain language and easily identifiable to the layperson. Incidentally, a lack of fee disclosure is one of the biggest reasons people leave their current advisor, followed by lack of contact.

Bottom Line: Portfolios should have some stock, some active funds, and some ETFs. This is the way to avoid the traps they all can present by themselves. In addition, such diversification protects you from being entirely impacted by any one investment's downside.

VARIABLE ANNUITIES
(NOT TO BE CONFUSED WITH
FIXED OR INDEXED ANNUITIES)

A variable annuity is more or less an insurance contract that is wrapped around some kind of investment, frequently a mutual fund. This means that they will have the same expenses we find in mutual funds. However, there is even more to consider when evaluating a variable annuity. There are two primary categories of annuities. Fixed annuities (including index annuities) are the first category and variable annuities are the second. In a way, "variable annuities" give annuities collectively a bad name. When you think about it, a variable annuity is just the opposite of the fixed annuity. The first annuity concept originated as a safe, tax-deferred investment vehicle, one that paid a pension for life. The variable annuity stripped the safety feature out of the traditional annuity by linking returns of the annuity to the market instead of protecting from it.

To properly evaluate a variable annuity, you must take the four mutual fund evaluation components we just discussed and add yet another expense. Variable annuities have a "mortality and expense fee" (M&E), typically around 1.25 percent, in addition to all the other fees we discussed associated with mutual funds. What does the M&E fee do? It pays a higher value when you die. It's like buying the most expensive insurance policy available. For example, if your variable annuity has a death benefit of $105,000, and your surrender value is $100,000 (which your family would get anyway upon your death) the variable annuity owner is paying over 1 percent per year, each and every year, on the entire account for only $5,000 more of a death benefit than is available anyway. M&E costs are associated with the most expensive life insurance in the world. A variable annuity used for an IRA is even more ludicrous. Think about it. All of these fees and life insurance costs on an IRA? Who needs that? It's not illegal, but it is inappropriate, in my opinion.

Sadly, in the twenty-six years I've been a financial advisor, I've never had anyone come to my office with a variable annuity who was actually told the complete truth about the related expenses when they purchased it. Many were told it was some sort of "market protection," but that's not really true. Your heart has to stop for that "market protection" to become effective. It is basically buying a very expensive life insurance policy on the little bit of gain you may derive from your variable annuity.

Again, one of the worst scenarios is when someone has a variable annuity inside of an IRA. They are paying insurance costs in a retirement account, plus the increased annual expenses from variable annuity fees, and with no additional tax benefits— after all, since an IRA is already tax-deferred, there is no additional benefit from owning an also-tax-deferred variable annuity within the account.

In summary and to restate: The variable annuity has a tax deferral benefit just like a fixed annuity. However, it's really in the market. It has all the basic mutual fund costs associated with it, as well as the M&E fees.

The bottom line is this, if you want to be in the market, be in the market. But look at alternatives that are lean, liquid, and low in expenses. By using indexing or structured market funds, it is possible to out-perform 80 to 90 percent of all active fund managers. Let me stipulate that again. It's a fact that over 80 to 90 percent (depending on which study you look at) of active mutual fund managers, who are paid millions, cannot even beat the basic indices.[3] If they are not meeting or beating the market, and you also have the fees and expenses we previously discussed, how productive will that mutual fund or variable annuity investment be for you?

If you want to be in the market, I will show you how to be in the market without incurring runaway costs, fees, and turnover charges. These are things that are usually not explained to the public. When I go through an initial discovery phase with a potential client, it is often the first time in their life they have seen the complete truth regarding the costs of their current investments. Usually, when they discover how much money they have been losing unnecessarily in their investments, they are open to considering an alternative that will be more productive. Unfortunately, they realize how much money has been taken from them in their previous investments, which they will never be able to recover.

If you know these costs are taking place, and you choose to be involved with a particular investment product, then that is simply a choice you make. However, if you don't know about the expenses and costs associated with the investment product, then there's something ethically wrong with being sold that type of

---

[3] Mark J. Perry. aei.org. October 18, 2018. "More evidence that it's really hard to 'beat the market' over time, 95% of finance professionals can't do it."
http://www.aei.org/publication/more-evidence-that-its-really-hard-to-beat-the-market-over-time-95-of-finance-professionals-cant-do-it/

product. I've talked to hundreds of people over the past twenty years and, unfortunately, this is a common tale for investors.

In summary, mutual funds have a series of listed expenses. Variable annuities have 3 to 5 percent annual expenses. Some may be higher than others. You really don't know what the expenses are until you look at a report that actually discloses all this information. I've explained turnover and how turnover can greatly impact your money and increase your expenses, but these expenses are not made transparent to you by a salesman. Because these things have not been disclosed to you directly, you're not being protected. I like to simply show people the truth and let them determine what is right for them. We also discussed variable annuities and their related expenses. They have even bigger expenses when you add the insurance costs.

These high-expense variable annuities and mutual funds are not the only game in town. There are plenty of ways one can make much greater returns with less cost and more tax efficiency.

If someone like Warren Buffett cares about how much his expenses are in his investments, then why should we treat our money any differently?

Chapter 5

DIVIDEND-PAYING STOCKS AND DRIPS

DIVIDENDS CAN COME IN THE FORM OF CASH OR SHARES OF STOCK

Before discussing dividend-paying stocks and DRIPs, it is critical to understand the meaning of "total return." Total return is simply defined as the total amount of money a particular investment has yielded over a specific period of time from a combination of the dividends, if paid out, and then the net gain or loss on a stock's value. For example, if you earned a 2 percent cash or stock dividend and your stock went up 1 percent, your total return is 3 percent. The combination of these two factors, measured over a specific period of time, will give you the "total return" on your stock. A stock can yield a dividend, yet still go down in price. This results in a lower net total return. As you can see, there are always variables that impact your total return; this chapter will help you identify various factors at play in an investment's total return.

Let's also define "blue chip stock." The term "blue chip" was derived from casinos and the game of poker where the blue chips are identified as the most valuable chips on the table. Blue chip stocks are stocks of large, well-established, financially sound companies that have operated for many years. A company that is considered blue chip typically has a market capitalization in the billions, is generally a market leader, is among the top three companies in its sector, and is often a household name.

While paying dividends is not absolutely necessary for a stock to be considered blue chip, most blue chips have a record of paying stable or rising dividends for years if not decades. They are traditionally thought to be a "safe" investment. The word "safe" is thrown around inappropriately about lots of things when it comes to the investing world, like gold. Blue chip stocks and gold for instance, are not likely to go down to zero, but they sure can fall below your principal or original investment at any time, so "safe" is still not a good descriptor. I want the reader to never forget that a blue-chip stock is still an equity-based investment and there is no equity-based investment that is safe or principal-protected. Yet, blue chip companies are thought to be in excellent financial shape and firmly entrenched as leaders in their respective fields.

DIVIDEND-PAYING STOCKS

Growth companies do not typically pay dividends, because profits and retained earnings are plowed back into growth-oriented activities, as opposed to paying out some profits or retained earnings in the form of cash or stock dividends to the equity holders. The main characteristic of blue-chip stocks is they generally pay dividends. Keep in mind, companies are not required to pay out dividends. But once a company starts paying dividends, missing a quarterly dividend could prove disastrous for its perceived value and stability. A company that stops or greatly reduces dividends from prior levels will get hammered in the stock market. Some companies have gotten away with lowering dividends, such as General Electric (GE). GE cut its dividend after the financial meltdown in 2007 to 2008. And indeed, the stock did get beaten up in the short-term.

Dividends are typically paid quarterly and are favorably regarded by investors because they are considered reliable. Investors can count on their dividends for income or to help get a consistent yield on their equities. Some examples of blue-chip stocks include well-known companies such as Wal-Mart, Coca-Cola, General Electric, and Exxon Mobile.

One of the measures of how the market is valuing a particular stock is its dividend yield. The math equation to calculate the dividend yield is to take the stock's annual payout and divide it by its share price. A stock's projected dividend over the next three years (known as a PEG Ratio) greatly affects the stock's valuation and can be used to determine if a stock is currently undervalued or overvalued.

A dividend yield that is high compared to interest rates on bonds is often the sign of a real bargain. At the time of writing of this book, the dividend yield of the average stock is, in fact, very high compared to the interest rate on U.S. government bonds. At the very least, as of the writing of this book, yields indicate stocks offer a better value than bonds, and investors are missing a good deal if they ignore that signal. The best way to exploit this situation is to purchase a solid company that pays a consistent dividend. Consider Colgate-Palmolive with the trading symbol "CL." As you know, they are a consumer-product giant and maker of toothpaste, deodorant, detergent, and many other products. They have paid big dividends without interruption since 1895 and have increased their payout annually for the past forty-seven years. At a share price of $74, the stock currently yields a 2.8 percent dividend. If you think that's low, think again. A ten-year Treasury note, as of May 2019, has yielded just 2.47 percent and a five-year treasury note is only 2.26 percent.[4]

DOW JONES INDUSTRIAL AVERAGE

A market index is designed to track the performance of a specific group of stocks that are considered to represent a particular market sector. There are indices (plural for index) for every conceivable sector of the economy. The most commonly used indices include the Dow Jones Industrial Average (DJIA), New York Stock Exchange (NYSE) Composite Index, S&P 500 Composite Stock Price Index, Wilshire 500 Total Market Index, Russell 2000® Index, and Nasdaq-100 Index.

The Dow Jones Industrial Average (DJIA) consists of the common stock of thirty blue chip stock companies such as Exxon Mobil, Verizon, General Electric, etc. You can refer to the table at the end of this section for a complete list of DJIA companies. One of the best places to look for a dividend-paying blue-chip company is in the DJIA. As mentioned before, these are usually solid companies that are leaders in their industry and considered

---

[4] US Department of The Treasury. May 10, 2019. "Daily Treasury Yield Curve Rates."
https://www.treasury.gov/resource-center/data-chart-center/interest-rates/Pages/TextView.aspx?data=yield

to be a lower risk than the rest of the market. However, again I will stress that it should be understood that no stock is "safe." It is worth noting that all thirty companies composing this index paid an average of 2.7 percent as a dividend since June 8, 2012. Among them, Proctor and Gamble and 3M Corporation, have boosted their dividends each year for at least fifty years.

A common investor mistake is staring at the DJIA ticker and assuming their portfolio is performing about the same. A Dalbar study shows investor returns do not come close to outperforming the indices due to fees and bad timing decisions.[5] Remember, the indices such as the DJIA or S&P 500 just reflect the organic movement of the underlying investments—they are not subject to management themselves, and don't reflect timing or expense variables that people have to consider in the real world. So, don't be misled.

To the untrained eye, the Dow can be a very deceptive index. It is a very narrow index and is only large-cap. Since there are only thirty stocks that make up the Dow, and they are pretty much blue chip stocks, this index is not representative of the stock market as a whole. The fact that the DJIA is not a value-based index such as the S&P can give an investor an inaccurate picture of the market. Value-weighted indices like the S&P 500 offer a better view of the market as a whole because, by tracking 500 stocks instead of just fifty, they offer a broader cross section of companies and industries.

---

[5] Dalbar. March 25, 2019. "Average Investor blown away by market turmoil in 2018."
https://www.dalbar.com/Portals/dalbar/Cache/News/PressReleases/
QAIBPressRelease_2019.pdf

The S&P 500 is indeed value-weighted, meaning larger companies are weighted in the formula calculating the index. Comparatively, the Dow Jones is simply taking the total amount of gain or loss for the day or any given moment and dividing it by thirty (the number of companies represented in the index). An index that is weighted is always going to be a more accurate indicator of the market it represents. The S&P 500 is probably the index watched most by the majority of investors because it represents the largest portion of the biggest publicly traded companies in the United States domestic market.

Yet, for those who are most interested in dividend-paying blue-chip stocks, the DJIA still offers a good look at the prices of the securities within the index, even though it doesn't account for stock or cash dividend payments. Following is a table of all the blue-chip companies composing the Dow.

Table of blue-chip companies that compose the Dow Jones Industrial Average:

Company Name	Ticker	Sector
3M Co.	MMM	Diversified Industrials
Alcoa Inc.	AA	Aluminum
American Express Co.	AXP	Consumer Finance
AT&T Inc.	T	Fixed Line Telecommunications
Bank of America Corp.	BAC	Banks
Boeing Co.	BA	Aerospace
Caterpillar Inc.	CAT	Commercial Vehicles & Trucks

Company Name	Ticker	Sector
Chevron Corp.	CVX	Integrated Oil & Gas
Citigroup Inc.	C	Banks
Coca-Cola Co.	KO	Soft Drinks
E.I. DuPont de Nemours & Co.	DD	Commodity Chemicals
Exxon Mobil Corp.	XOM	Integrated Oil & Gas
General Electric Co.	GE	Diversified Industrials
General Motors Corp.	GM	Automobiles
Hewlett-Packard Co.	HPQ	Computer Hardware
Home Depot Inc.	HD	Home Improvement Retailers
Intel Corp.	INTC	Semiconductors
International Business Machines Corp.	IBM	Computer Services
Johnson & Johnson	JNJ	Pharmaceuticals
JPMorgan Chase & Co.	JPM	Banks
Kraft Foods Inc. Cl A	KFT	Food Products
McDonald's Corp.	MCD	Restaurants & Bars
Merck & Co. Inc.	MRK	Pharmaceuticals
Microsoft Corp.	MSFT	Software
Pfizer Inc.	PFE	Pharmaceuticals
Procter & Gamble Co.	PG	Nondurable Household Products
United Technologies Corp.	UTX	Aerospace
Verizon Communications Inc.	VZ	Fixed Line Telecommunications
Wal-Mart Stores Inc.	WMT	Broadline Retailers
Walt Disney Co.	DIS	Broadcasting & Entertainment

PREFERRED STOCK

Blue chip companies (and any company, for that matter) can issue two types of stock: common and preferred stock. Common stock is what you see in the Dow Jones Industrial Average and in other indices such as the S&P 500. Preferred shares are another type of issue considered less volatile than the sister blue chip common stock, but they are still an equity and they can go up or down in value. There are four types of preferred stock:

- **Cumulative** – Shareholders are paid missed preferred dividends before the dividends are paid on common stock.
- **Non-cumulative** – Shareholders are not paid missed dividends.
- **Participating** – Shareholders receive regular fixed dividends, plus an additional dividend if the common stock dividend exceeds a specified amount.
- **Convertible** – Shareholders can convert preferred shares into a specified number of common shares.

Preferred shares are higher on the food chain than common stock when it comes to dividends. That is, preferred stock dividends are paid out before common stock dividends. Preferred stock is often used in income portfolios for investors. With a preferred stock, you have a chance for some capital appreciation, but you typically will receive a reliable dividend for the preferred shares you own. Not every company that is traded in the exchanges also has preferred shares to offer investors. You have to look for the companies that offer preferred stock and they are not hard to find. A quick inquiry on any reliable internet search engine should give you a list of companies that offer preferred stock.

Preferred stock pays dividends subject to declaration by the corporation. Dividends are paid on a certain percentage of the par value of the stock. Preferred share dividends must be satisfied before a company can pay dividends to holders of common stock. A company doesn't have to pay dividends, but once it starts paying dividends it tends not to stop paying dividends, because it doesn't want to give investors the wrong or negative impression about the company. Dividends can also be issued as additional shares of stock in the company. Preferred stock holders also get preferential treatment over common stock holders in the case of a company bankruptcy or liquidation. Typically, those buying preferred shares are corporations and individuals looking for a steady flow of income. Preferred stock can also be used as a bond proxy or substitute in a portfolio, often when bonds are expected to be volatile or low yielding.

DIVIDEND REINVESTMENT PLAN (DRIPS)

A Dividend Reinvestment Plan is commonly referred to as a DRIP. The concept behind the DRIP is actually very simple. Instead of having the dividend distributed to you personally, you just opt to automatically reinvest all the dividends back into the stock to purchase more shares.

Some investors like this option because you don't need a broker to do this and you don't have to pay a broker's fee. If you own the stock in a company, you can simply ask the company to reinvest all of your dividends rather than sending you a check for the dividends. Of course, you can also do this through an advisor or retail online account. Many financial advisors don't like it when people do this on their own, simply because it does not include the advisor. You should discuss this with your financial advisor to determine the best strategy for yourself.

DRIPs can be pretty effective. Keep in mind that you still have to pay tax each year on any dividends paid out by the stock company, even if you reinvest them. All dividends are taxable, whether or not you do a DRIP. DRIPs are very similar to dollar-cost averaging.

As you may already know, dollar-cost averaging is putting more money into the same investment on a regular basis, theoretically paying a lower average share price over time. But I stress the word *theoretically*. True dollar-cost averaging is purchasing shares on a consistent basis, whether the share price is up or down. This is what most people do when they invest in a 401(k) at work. It is definitely a smarter way to gradually invest, rather than saving up over time and then dumping your entire life savings into the market in one day and hoping that you purchased your stocks at an opportune time.

You can own a stock directly from a company and sign up for a DRIP arrangement. But you can also do this through an investment company by opening an account, such as with TD Ameritrade or Charles Schwab. Either will reinvest dividends with no transaction costs. These kinds of accounts put all your stocks in one reportable location for easy monitoring. These arrangements are much more convenient than owning each individual stock directly with each company.

PROPER DIVERSIFICATION

I would like to state again that buying appropriate stocks can be a good supplement to a properly diversified portfolio. I do not recommend having your whole life savings in a bunch of dividend-paying stocks, because you're not able to get much diversity. You can get better upside and lesser downside with an indexed core portfolio. I explain in a later chapter how to create a properly diversified portfolio using the seven-twelve method as your core, and then surrounding it with a measured percentage of dividend-paying stocks. I will stress again that stocks can pay a dividend, but they can also decrease in value even in years they pay dividends. Keep in mind, stocks contain risk. There's no absolute guarantee of your principal in any way, shape, or form.

Chapter 6

THE PRINCIPLES OF RISK AND YOUR RETIREMENT

Living at risk is like jumping off a cliff
and making your wings on the way down.
~Ray Bradbury

Risk comes from not knowing
what you are doing.
~Warren Buffet

The preceding quotes represent similar perceptions of risk. It has been interesting for me to see how people view risk after many meetings with clients over the past twenty years. My experience in working with individuals who have medium to large portfolios has led me to conclude that, outside of bad tax planning in retirement, unmonitored risk is the most common way to shrink one's wealth. This cold fact is even less forgiving as you get closer to retirement. At or near retirement, all conditions are magnified in their impact, both good and bad.

How much risk should you have *at* or *near* retirement?

As you know, the answer to that question will be somewhat different for each person. Each person is unique and has differing perceptions as well as various tolerances for risk.

There are a few prudent principles the pre- or post-retiree investor should know about. If they fear any risk to their future cost of living or to their future income streams, they should proceed with great caution. Interestingly enough, both the modestly wealthy and the very wealthy retirees have similar concerns about outliving their money.

With life expectancy now routinely reaching the late eighties to mid-nineties and the rising cost of living, retirees now, more than ever, risk outliving their money if they are not careful.

Following are six principles that will serve as a 20/20 guide to protecting the life of your money.

PRINCIPLE 1

Accept this axiom wholeheartedly:
When a person is at or near retirement,
they become a different investor than they were
before, whether they realize it or not.

In order for the following principles to make sense, you must be reasonable enough to agree with the preceding statement. If not, many more mistakes will be made going forward that may hinder your cause. You see, during your younger working years you are in what is called the "accumulation stage" of your investment life. When you are at or near retirement, you are in the "harvesting/preservation stage" of your investment life.

The two stages are very, very different.

The accumulation stage is just that. Save as much as possible, invest wisely, and stay in for the long haul. That's it. You can now add employer matches and long-term growth over a thirty-five to forty-year period.

Once you reach your fifties, you become different than you were before. As time ticks on, we all have less and less runway to recover from mistakes before retirement. You still stick to the principles of growth and accumulation, but now you have to add tax-harvesting, ratcheted-down risk, and most importantly *income* planning.

This last third of your life (hopefully a long third) can last *twenty to thirty years* if you live long enough. The length of time you have left in the harvesting stage undeniably magnifies the impact of financial mistakes.

The harvesting stage has another unique factor that cannot be overlooked, which is in great contrast to the accumulation stage. This stage has the unknown, inevitable, and unpredictable challenge of failing physical and mental acuity. Most people recognize the fact that they are a different investor at or near retirement simply because of time, and they don't have time to wait for markets to recover large losses. However, you must also acknowledge that you may not always have the ability to make decisions due to diminished mental capacity.

As an investor and professional advisor, I sure do not want to spend my retirement watching CNBC or staring at the market ticker with worry. I will have someone manage my affairs just like you should.

Unfortunately, as we age, many people are not able to reason or handle stressful financial decisions as clearly as they did in their younger years. Judgment can be impaired when it comes to making risk decisions. As one becomes older, it is a good rule-of-thumb to try to keep some of your finances going in the direction of more simplicity rather than complexity. It makes sense, yes?

After personally meeting with several hundred investors, I have found people who can come to terms with the first principle are more successful and happier in retirement. They have less stress than those who continue to be in denial of this reality.

PRINCIPLE 2

Observe the Rule of 100

The Rule of 100 is a simple way to determine if you are even in the ballpark of where you should be with your ratio of risk money to "safe" money. This rule is very simple. You just take the number 100 and subtract your age. The remaining number is the maximum percentage of assets you should have in risk-based investments with the potential to lose money. For example, if you're seventy years old, you would subtract seventy from 100. The answer, thirty, represents the maximum percentage amount you should have in risk-based investments. In this example, 30 percent is how much risk you should have at that stage of your life. If you are trying to factor this for a couple, just take the average of the two ages and subtract *that* number from 100. I realize this is not a scientific method. But it does still make sense. We use more detailed metrics when we advise people about their investments. However, it is still a good indicator to determine if you have the proper amount at risk for your age, at least, to know if you are in the ballpark.

100 minus your age = percentage of assets you should have in at-risk investments

PRINCIPLE 3

Do not confuse bond income funds with "safety" or "guarantee of principle"

One of the most common misunderstandings is people's misguided belief that a fixed income fund is the same as a safe, principle-protected financial tool. The truth is that bond income funds (do not confuse with ownership of actual, individual bonds) can lose value just like any other mutual fund.

In 2008, fixed income funds melted down with the rest of the fund universe and offered no safe haven whatsoever. Some went down drastically. Bond *funds* are not safe. They are just considered a more *conservative* balance in an equity/bond portfolio. Do not be among those who make this mistake. A lot of folks had a rude awakening about bond funds during the Great Recession of 2008, and they will never forget that again. Now, fast forward ten-plus years to low interest rates. Such rates position bonds as the next bubble to be considered a financial threat. You see, bond yields have an inverse relationship to interest rates. When interest rates have nowhere to go but up, what does that mean? It means bond yields have nowhere to go but down. In a mutual bond fund, you will get smashed. This is because bond funds have no maturities, specified income stream, no return of principal, and after big fund outflows, those who stay in the bond fund will be greatly damaged for it. Their values will drop significantly. In bond funds or any mutual fund, your ongoing loyalty by staying in the fund is rewarded with punishment.

If you own an actual bond and not a bond fund, you will not lose your principal, assuming the individual company does not go bankrupt. Your bond's coupon payment will still come every six months, and barring a company bankruptcy, you will get your original principal back at maturity. The calculated yield will dip with the rest in the interim, but you will not realize the loss unless you redeem the bond prior to maturity.

What is guaranteed?

The only items that are absolutely guaranteed are government-backed securities such as Treasury bills, notes, and bonds. Treasury Inflation Protected Securities (TIPS), Ginnie Maes, and Freddie Macs are also backed by the full faith and credit of the U.S. government. Other guaranteed vehicles are CDs and savings accounts at banks that are FDIC-insured up to $250,000. Also, fixed and indexed annuities can be added to this list of safe options. These are called guaranteed insurance contracts, or GICs (this list is not exhaustive). GICs are backed by the financial strength of the issuing insurance company itself. All of the preceding categories are the only truly safe instruments that are guaranteed by some institution or authority. So, don't make the mistake by thinking if you are invested in a fixed-income fund, you are not in the market. That is absolutely not true.

Anything that is a "fund," unless it is a fund that has only government guaranteed contracts, can go down in value.

PRINCIPLE 4

Have recurring risk discussions with a qualified financial advisor

The basis of this principle is many people do not even participate in a risk discussion at all. Some only get a risk assessment in the beginning of a relationship with an advisor. However, risk discussions should be recurring throughout your investment life. We all face transitions in life such as age, financial status, ability to work, our goals . . . the list can go on and on. Any life change can affect your financial plan, which is why you must stay in touch with your financial team on a regular basis.

This doesn't actually start with your advisor. The risk discussion actually begins with trying to understand yourself as best you can. You need to have a recurring conversation with yourself. How do you really feel about risk? Do you really understand risk? Do you understand that not all financial investments are equal in risk? After an introspective conversation with yourself, you should continue the dialogue with a qualified financial advisor to adjust your investment portfolio and make it reflective of your changing risk tolerance.

There are many studies that show there is not an equal amount of emotion when you lose 20 percent in the market as compared to gaining 20 percent in the market. In other words, the joy of the gain is not equally as deep as the pain of loss. Studies show that people feel loss far more emotionally, and for a longer duration than they do with wins. Make sure your investments reflect you . . . The real you![6]

PRINCIPLE 5

Avoid the equally dangerous overdiversification, or the redundancy portfolio

On one end of the spectrum, having only one or two asset classes represented in your portfolio can be a very risky proposition. But a portfolio with too many positions can be just as risky with your nest egg. I am describing two extremes that have equal dangers to you.

Allow me to explain. I can't tell you how many $200,000 and $400,000 portfolios I have reviewed over the years that have fifty and sixty stock positions in just large-cap funds. People will say, "Well, I have different industries across the large-cap asset class." That is true. But they are all "large-cap assets," and therefore, under-diversified. It is a nightmare to analyze these "haystack" or "linguini" portfolios. Very often such investors own positions that have only $1,500 to $2,000 in each position. Often, I find these positions originate with a large brokerage firm, where you can find most people who walk out of the front door have near-identical portfolios despite having very different lives and goals.

The reasoning behind the haystack or linguini portfolio is to throw enough large-cap funds on the wall, for then, something is bound to make money. Or, so a client can't sue the advisor for

---

[6] Amos Tversky and Daniel Kahneman. Oxford Journals. 1991. "Loss Aversion in Riskless Choice."
http://www.sscnet.ucla.edu/polisci/faculty/chwe/austen/tversky1991.pdf

having money in the case of another Enron, let's just put a million stocks in one portfolio. I call this over-diversified financial plan a "linguini portfolio," because if you throw enough linguini on the wall, some of it is going to stick. But, most of it is going to fall to the ground. I feel these linguini portfolios display a lack of education, conviction, and ideas. I suspect these designs may even be legally motivated; if you have eight million different stocks, it may be harder to sue an advisor for losses.

The linguini portfolio is typically in a bunch of large-cap stocks, even though they are often in multiple industries such as medical, agricultural, etc. The rising tide raises all boats in a certain asset class, but it can also sink all the boats. In a down market, what do you sell? You want to have yourself in the right amount of asset classes, but not in so many that you are spread thin. You don't want to be so out of whack that you risk getting wiped out by the next inevitable market cycle playing itself out.

Actually, you should be able to explain your portfolio design in one or two sentences. A good succinct description would be, "My accounts are comprised of all twelve asset classes in over forty countries and are rebalanced quarterly." It can be as simple as that. There is no way to accurately and succinctly describe a linguini portfolio, except maybe, "I have a linguini portfolio."

This leads us to the question, when is too much diversification really just too much, and nothing more than duplication and redundancy? If you have a $200,000 portfolio with fifty stocks in it, which is very common, and one of them goes up 10 percent, what impact is that really making in a positive way in your portfolio? Especially when twenty others have gone down? Or, when the market is making a huge correction, like it does periodically as part of its nature, what do you sell? You're going to face a lot of transaction costs to get rid of the stocks while trying to reduce your risk exposure.

The linguini portfolio screams of an advisor who doesn't want to take responsibility for any kind of choices within their design. Just having more "stuff" does not create proper diversification. So, avoid the linguini portfolio because it can be just as damaging as an under-diversified portfolio. It is an extreme. And we know extremes do not last very long. In the next chapter, I will explain how you can attempt to gain optimal diversification.

PRINCIPLE 6

Use assets with low and zero correlation to reduce downside and improve upside

People often conclude that if they have reduced the downside, they are automatically achieving upside potential. I can tell you without a doubt this is utterly untrue. First, let's explore the meaning of "correlation," for those who are not familiar with quantitative or statistical analysis. The range here is from -1 to +1. Those two ends of the spectrum represent the maximum difference between two investments. In other words, if something is equally correlated, that is, if you have one investment that is exactly the same as another investment in the same asset class, they will have a +1 relationship or correlation with each other. Whereas, an investment that is exactly the opposite in correlation to another investment will have a -1 relationship. You don't want half of your portfolio to be +1s and the other half to be -1s, because one set of investments will be going up and the other set will be going down by the same amount all the time. You would always have a draw. That wouldn't make a lot of sense. What you should be trying to accomplish is to get your assets as close to zero (in between -1 and +1) as possible.

It's not effective to have too many of the same things. Many people have mutual funds or stocks that are all large-cap, but that's only one of twelve asset classes. This person's portfolio is going to live and die with the overall performance of large-cap stocks. If you think back to the Great Recession, when stock market values from 2001 to 2010 might as well have flatlined, having all of the same kind of assets (all losing value or more or less staying the same) wouldn't have been much help. The goal is to have assets that have less and less relation to one another. An example would be having a Guaranteed Insurance Contract (GIC) (or, fixed index annuity) in relationship to your stock portfolio. There is absolutely zero correlation between the GIC and the market. They are both very different. You can also go further to improve the asset balance in your equity portfolio. You can have exposure to all twelve asset classes, at all times, so you don't get the big drawdowns and you do not have to chase trends. Believe it or not, statistics show that with the right sweet spot of diversification, you can actually have higher upside compared to downside.

CONCLUSION

Once you have clearly understood and calibrated your risk-versus-safe-money ratio, you can ignore all the financial fear-mongering you hear and the plethora of television and radio advertisements that guide you to their supposed solution.

There is a continuous flow of radio advertising leading you to believe that things such as gold will bullet-proof your IRA. Bullet-proof? Really? These commercials are simply misleading and should be censored. In my opinion, the SEC is very overwhelmed and slimmed down, else these shysters wouldn't be on TV. Again, this is my opinion, but the SEC does not enforce enough existing regulations to protect investors. The SEC and Congress failed to protect investors from the frauds of the 1980s and 1990s, as well as the most recent cataclysmic market events.

I will get off my soapbox now and finish this chapter with one thought. By balancing risk, you can be both a long-term investor *and* a bird-in-the-hand investor at the same time.

A balanced, hybrid approach to risk and income sources puts you in the position of not having to bet that you are right. It puts you in the camp of just betting you won't be wrong. Think about it. Low correlation between your assets can be done very easily, so you do not need to be a rocket scientist.

For any overly technical aspects of this book, I apologize. Hopefully I've adequately explained some of the more in-depth concepts—it's important that you have at least a basic understanding of how your nest egg can be built and protected.

I think you absolutely should have a trusted financial advisor who takes care of the particulars, but you need to be armed with enough knowledge to look out for yourself and be sure whomever you're working with is acting in line with your goals.

When it comes to correlation, you want each piece of your nest egg to have a measured difference from the others in terms ofc behavior, quality, and cycles. This will help you keep more of the market upside and avoid taking steep dives when the market hits a down cycle.

Chapter 7

EXCHANGE-TRADED FUNDS (ETFS) AND INDEXING

*Attempting to forecast whether the market is at a peak
or in a valley—and whether to buy or sell stocks as a result—
is a waste of time. I don't know anyone
who has been right more than once in a row.
~Legendary Investor Peter Lynch*

*After fifty years in the business, I do not know of anybody
who has done it (market timing) successfully and consistently.
I do not even know anybody who knows anybody
who has done it successfully and consistently.
~John Bogle, Founder, Vanguard Funds*

Efficient markets mean they represent all available information at any given time, simultaneously. It means the market itself is going to perform better than any metric indicator, any predictive mechanism, or any guess at future performance.

According to Nobel Prize Winner Harry Markowitz's Efficient Market Hypothesis, the market's movements reflect all stock on a constant and continuous basis. In other words, there is little or no proven ability to anticipate the future movement of a stock or the market itself.

Because we have such efficient markets and cannot hope to beat the market with any consistency, we just need to parallel the market. This is why low costs and indexing can provide more than sufficient returns to outpace inflation.

What is the difference between actively managed funds and indexing, or index funds?

In recent years, exchange-traded funds (ETF) gained great popularity among savvy investors, approaching $5 trillion in assets.[7] The traditional mutual fund's efficacy is being greatly challenged by the growing ETF movement. Because there are distinct advantages to ETFs as compared to mutual funds, ETFs take an index-related approach to investing, whereas most mutual funds are actively managed by money managers. These managers use their own judgment and experience to make deliberate choices about which investments to include in a particular fund. Part of Mark Matson's ($4 billion under management) philosophy about Wall Street bullies speaks to active management. He explains how these gurus always want

---

[7] Ryan Vlastelica. MarketWatch. January 3, 2018. "ETFs shattered their growth records in 2017."
https://www.marketwatch.com/story/etfs-shattered-their-growth-records-in-2017-2017-12-11

you to think they are smarter than you. I can tell you firsthand that they are dead wrong!

You may be interested to know that *over 90 percent of actively managed funds do not beat the market.*[8] Furthermore, active mutual funds have both visible and invisible fees, costs, and charges. The small percentage of most active managers that beat the market in a given year or years do so simply by luck, buoyed by the performance of the core asset class. In other words, many people get sucked into the 10 percent of funds that have beaten the market and make the mistake of buying into a fund based on its past returns. This is called chasing returns. The value of funds *will* pivot downward when money starts to flow out of the asset class. Funds that do well for a year or two are largely due to the cyclical nature of various asset classes. I strongly recommend you do not get caught in this trap.

What Is Indexing?

The late John Bogle, one of the founders of Vanguard, held a long-time belief of not fighting the efficiency of the market with active trend-following or stock-picking. He asserts in several books that active management is for the birds. He, others, and I believe in three primary principles:

1. Keep your investment costs low.
2. Indexing beats active stock-picking. (Markets make money. People don't!)

---

[8] Mark J. Perry. aei.org. Oct. 18, 2018. "More evidence that it's really hard to 'beat the market' over time, 95% of finance professionals can't do it." http://www.aei.org/publication/more-evidence-that-its-really-hard-to-beat-the-market-over-time-95-of-finance-professionals-cant-do-it/

3. Don't chase asset classes. Be in most of them at the same time and rebalance.

John Bogle was one of the originators of the first indexed mutual funds at Vanguard. These indexed funds were low in costs, had little turnover, and were 100 percent transparent. They also tended to out-perform most active funds, and still often do today. Those first "indexed" mutual funds were the precursor to what we now know as an ETF, or exchange-traded fund.

What Exactly Is an ETF?

An ETF is like a basket of stocks in one position. An S&P 500 ETF does not have all 500 stocks in it. But it has a chosen sample group to represent the index.

A small-cap index may have the 2,000 small companies from the Russell 2000 index. There are thousands of ETFs out there now to index to nearly anything. For example, if you want to index gold, you can buy a gold ETF. If you want to include a China index, one ETF can satisfy this with a multi-industry China index. ETFs are simple, visible, and tax efficient.

Here is a sample list of single ETF asset classes:

1. Large-, mid-, small-, and micro-cap
2. Currencies
3. Precious metals
4. Countries (Brazil, China, Japan, etc.)
5. Bonds
6. Inverted (they go up when an index goes down)
7. Commodities (gold, silver, oil, wheat, cattle, etc.)

8. Industry groups (technology, durable goods, consumer staples, biotech, etc.)
9. Natural resources

Another important point about ETFs is they trade in real time like stocks. You can use charts to assist in better entries and exits. Mutual funds do not have charts and they are priced only once per business day at 5:30 p.m. Eastern.

How Do I Know What ETFs to Buy?

Before you look for specific ETFs, you need to settle on an objective or design of a portfolio, or, more plainly, you must decide on the allocation of your assets, which means how much you have within an asset class and where.

Is the Track Record of an ETF Important?

Not by itself, no. Because if you see a negative return on an ETF over some arbitrary time period, it simply means that sector, asset class, or segment of the market just experienced the inevitable cyclical downside. *There is no management error for one to judge in an ETF.*

The history of an ETF is basically irrelevant. The history is a history of an asset class, not a management company. Why is this so? Because, an ETF should be used with others in a portfolio. You do not want all of your investments to go up or down all at the same time. That would be terrible risk management and an opportunity cost, as well.

As I have said, every asset class has its day in the sun and its day in the rain. Even professionals cannot predict asset class cycles consistently. One does not know that something is a strong positive or strong negative trend until it is in your rear-view mirror. That is why passive indexing across all asset classes eliminates the inevitable human error in trying to time or predict trends. It is as simple as that. How do you match or beat the market? You *become* the market and rebalance. That's it.

What Are the Costs in an ETF?

Exchange-traded funds have no loads or commissions. That is why working with a fee-based advisor saves you money each and every year. If nothing else, the strict paring down of hidden costs directionally aids positive returns. This is assuming, of course, that the fee-based advisor is not charging more than 1.4 percent in total costs. On the other hand, loaded, or commission-based mutual funds cost investors plenty. ETF annual charges are pretty low, usually less than one-half of 1 percent. If you work with a fee-based advisor charging 1 percent to manage your portfolio, your total investment costs should not exceed 1.4 percent per year (ETF annual costs included).

On the other hand, the average mutual fund holder has 2 percent or higher annual fees. Realistically, your costs in a mutual fund or variable annuity can be as high as 3 to 5 percent per year.

Are ETFs Tax-Efficient?

ETFs are more tax efficient than active mutual funds. They do not create phantom income tax and the capital gains are deferred like a stock, until you decide to trigger the capital gain, which means more control for you. Also, dividends from ETFs may receive preferential tax treatment like stocks.[9]

Do you Have More Control in an ETF or an Active Mutual Fund?

The empowerment for investors in ETFs begins and ends with transparency. When you invest in an ETF, you know exactly what and where your money is at all times. If you have a position in the S&P 500 Index ETF, then you know exactly where your money is invested, and you can see it clearly. Lack of transparency in active mutual funds is a growing problem for investors. People want, and should have, more transparency about where their money is positioned and what the costs are in their portfolio.

Another investor empowerment from ETFs comes in the form of being able to slowly construct a new portfolio over time. You do not want your money to be invested all in one day. If you do, you run the short-term risk of getting "whip- sawed" in the short-term by market volatility. A portfolio should be built like a house, with one ETF foundation block at a time. Conversely, if the market is melting down and you want to reduce your exposure, you can remove some of the more volatile pieces.

Did you ever wonder why a commission-based advisor plunks you in all of the mutual funds in one day? The answer is simple. The advisor does not get paid until your funds are invested in the market. The commissioned broker, from the start, is putting all

---

[9] Jeff Brown. U.S. News & World Report. *Beware of Phantom Income and the Tax It Brings.*
https://money.usnews.com/investing/investing-101/articles/2018-07-09/beware-of-phantom-income-and-the-tax-it-brings

your money in the market in one day, even if it might be the worst day of the month or year to commit your life savings to the market.

Have you ever wondered why you get so much attention from a commission-based advisor in the beginning and then you get less and less attention as time goes on? This phenomenon occurs because the advisor has already made his money off you and receives little or no recurring income annually. Think about it! Where would you put your attention if you were them? Strictly "new business," that's where.

A Final Word on Exchange-Traded Funds:

ETFs are why the more discerning advisors are able to keep their clients' costs and taxes under control. ETFs have negligible turnover in contrast to active mutual funds, they don't rely on active market timing, charge bare minimum costs, provide high tax efficiency, and are transparent. They are indexed-based and not dependent on market timing. Additionally, ETFs do not generate phantom income tax, or any other kind of runaway taxation. ETFs can receive preferential (lower) dividend-tax treatment, so they are great for non-IRA accounts due to their superior tax efficiency compared to active mutual funds.

Chapter 8
ANNUITIES
ARE THEY GOOD OR BAD?

"I have heard bad things about annuities…"
~Everyone

If you are a retiree or pre-retiree, you may have already been bombarded on a regular basis with annuity salespeople. Due to a high level of curiosity and the multitude of decisions required when approaching retirement, annuities continue to be a very hot topic these days. I caution you, reader, to not dismiss all annuities.

How many of you remember the Yugo automobile from Yugoslavia, which was introduced in the U.S. in the 1980s? It was such a poorly made vehicle at such a low cost that dealerships were practically giving away the Yugo when people bought a new Cadillac.[10] Yugo Motors quickly went out of business. Would you ever buy a car if all you researched about cars was material about a Yugo? The word "car" is a very

---

[10] Scripps Howard News Service. Chicago Tribune. March 22, 1986. *Buy a New Cadillac, Get a Yugo Thrown in Free.*
https://www.chicagotribune.com/news/ct-xpm-1986-03-22-8601210722-story.html

general term or classification of a thing, just like the word "annuity" is a general term covering a wide spectrum of good, bad, and the best of annuities. It is worth noting that institutions must create an enemy for when they take an us-versus-them approach to marketing.

Companies such as Fisher Investments hate all annuities because annuities are the single greatest competitor for them. It works vice versa, as well: the annuity-based people think annuities are the solution for everything. As fiduciaries for our clients, here at Alpha Planning, we block and tackle for them, and actually protect them from the big institutions and their extreme biases in one direction and another.

The best type of annuities, fixed index annuities, have low or zero expenses, market safety, and flexible income options. In short, they preserve your money and provide part of your total income when you need it.

In this chapter, I will hopefully clarify which types of annuities do what, which can be dismissed, and which deserve serious consideration. In fact, some people can do without any annuities at all in their retirement portfolio and their money will still outlive them.

Each individual should engage in a private series of meetings with a qualified financial advisor to determine the appropriateness of annuities for their portfolio.

I wish to be upfront with readers. In our firm, we not only manage market money, we also use annuities when appropriate, when they are a good fit, and when in the best interest of the client. However, there are certain types of annuities we do not use because of less-than-desirable features or conditions. I will describe the two types of annuities that are most popular in the retirement preparation world.[11] After you read it for yourself, then you be the judge. You will know by the end of this chapter which kind, if any, may be best suited for you and yours.

When all is said and done, you should consult with a professional before entering into any contract and be sure that whatever you're looking into fits within the overall context of your portfolio.

So, here are two main categories of annuities:

VARIABLE (VA) and FIXED INDEX (FIA)

Let's start with FIAs: Owners get half the market gains with no downside, or investment costs.

• Fixed index annuities are strictly insurance products. In the financial services industry, fixed annuities are also referred to as a "GIC" or Guaranteed Insurance Contract.

• Fixed index annuities are not invested in the market and are not subject to market risk or loss of principal. FIAs do not typically have any costs in their base products. These vehicles credit interest to the principal, adding to the principal each year.

---

[11] Greg Iacurci. Investment News. February 20, 2019. *Fixed annuity sales smash previous record.*
https://www.investmentnews.com/article/20190220/FREE/190229989/fixed-annuity-sales-smash-previous-record

• Some products have an option to choose an income rider, an enhanced death benefit rider, or a return of premium rider. These riders are entirely optional and the costs for the riders are usually quite minimal, usually less than 1 percent per year. There are no other costs or fees in the average FIA. I prefer zero costs and only opt for special riders in special situations.

An FIA is a contract through an insurance company in which someone pays the insurance company and then waits, often for ten years or so, for their contract to have time to increase in value. After the initial contract period, the insurance company begins paying the contract holder an income based on the contract's value.

Now, that time period where the contract value is growing is critical. It's called a fixed *index* annuity because the contract value is tied to a stock market index. Again, this is an insurance contract, your principal is protected by the full force of the insurance company, and you aren't *invested* in the index. But the insurance company credits your contract based on features like *caps* or *spreads* of an index like the S&P 500.

If your contract value is increasing based on a cap, say, 8 percent, it means that when the market is up, your FIA will also increase during that period up to the cap. If the market is up by 18 percent, you get 8 percent. But if the market is down 5 percent, your contract's value hasn't gone anywhere. A spread means that your credit will be the index value minus a certain percentage. So, say you have a 3 percent spread. If the S&P 500 makes 2 percent, you don't gain anything (you don't lose, either), but if the S&P 500 hits 20 percent, your contract will reach 18 percent.

These are just a few examples of the various crediting methods insurance companies use to attribute more value to your contract. The important things to know: 1. FIAs are insurance, not investments, therefore 2. your contract value may increase based on the index, but market performance *won't ever decrease your contract value.*

In an indexed annuity, you can even allocate your potential gains at no risk to your principal investment. Most contracts allow annuity holders to readjust their choices of interest or index options on every anniversary from the date the annuity was opened. So, you could theoretically (depending on the company that holds your contract) decide to use a capped crediting method one year or select a crediting method that represents a certain percentage of market gains.

Each company must offer a detailed statement of understanding to help a potential investor determine if any particular annuity is right for them. There are many designs and nuances with how each company credits or limits index gains.

Are FIAs Good for Wealth Accumulation?

They sure can be when balanced with a prudent market portfolio, which I explain in the following study. But first, it is worth noting that some FIAs are very good for accumulating funds, while other times an FIA may need a rider to ensure that lifetime income never runs out.

Once again, fixed annuities are the strongest for permanent income that never runs out. For folks who don't want to see their values decline, but who are interested in getting about half of the market's returns in positive years, FIAs can be a good proxy for a safe accumulation vehicle. You have principal protection with potential interest or index gains. These FIAs provided an oasis of sanity for clients in 2008 to 2009, when they did not lose one red cent in their contracts while the market burned down.

Instead of comparing indexed annuity returns with pure stock market returns, you should balance some stock market money for the long-term, while keeping other assets preserved and controlled with an FIA. The indexed annuity should be looked upon as an efficient substitute for the typical bond portfolio in retirement, a place to put money that you don't want to expose to risk while also seeking some return.

Zebra Capital® released a study in January 2018 by Roger G. Ibbotson, PhD, who conducted a verifiable study, "Fixed-Indexed Annuities: Consider the Alternative." This work compares indexed annuity returns by themselves, as well as the usual 60/40 stock/bond portfolio by itself, and then shows both together.[12]

Caveat: Please read the report in its entirety
if you doubt the efficacy of these excerpts.

In summary:

• Annualized three-year return on only FIA = **8.3 percent**
• Annualized three-year return on a 60 percent balanced stock portfolio only = **10.1 percent**

---

[12] Roger G. Ibbotson. Zebra Capital. January 2018. "Fixed Indexed Annuities: Consider the Alternative."
https://dta0yqvfnusiq.cloudfront.net/commo93759149/2018/02/Ibbotson-White-Paper-5a78d2dea0f40.pdf

• Annualized three-year return on a 60 percent balanced stock portfolio and 40 percent FIA = **15.3 percent**

Indexed annuities ensure your income withdrawals do not rob your market money when the market is down. They prevent the biggest cardinal sin in retirement: Taking income out during a bear market year. When (not if) that happens, money withdrawn in that environment is truly a lost opportunity cost.

On to our discussion of VAs . . .

VARIABLE ANNUITIES

Variable annuities, or VAs, are both an insurance product *and* a registered securities product. There are several important things you should know about them. Variable annuities (or VAs) *are invested in the market* and subject to loss as well as gain. VAs have heavy insurance and investment costs. Over the past twenty years, I have analyzed several hundred variable annuity contracts. I have found the average variable annuity has annual expenses of 3.5 percent, and I've seen variable annuities with as high as 5 percent of their values headed to fees each year. Yes, 5 percent.

Variable annuities are especially bad for IRAs. Paying insurance costs in an IRA is an awful idea. An IRA is primarily a tax-deferred wrapper to help you invest—it does not need insurance!

Following is a breakdown of the total costs that must be accounted for in any variable annuity.

Variable M&E Annual Cost

This is a mortality and expense fee, which the insurance company charges to assume the risk of insuring the death benefit portion of the variable annuity. This cost is usually at least 1.25 percent to 1.50 percent on the whole account each and every year. Although they use the term "M&E," this cost is simply just expensive life insurance.

Fund Costs

As I explained before, variable annuities are investments, unlike other kinds of annuities. Underlying the insurance wrapper, you'll find some kind of stock or investing product, usually mutual funds. Those investments come with their own fees. Remember the discussion of mutual funds and their various expenses? Well, in addition to other VA fees, you'll also have all of those mutual fund costs.

Turnover

Also related to our discussion of mutual funds, the more a variable annuity's portfolio changes, with managers selling and buying on the back end, you'll incur costs to your VA from the expenses of turnover.

Jeff, if you say VAs are so unfavorable, then why are billions of dollars put into them each year by some of the biggest financial companies?

The answer to that is shrouded in the "great deception" of Wall Street, only proven by the devastation wrought over the years on unsuspecting investors.

Just because a company is large does not mean it uses products or designs that are ideal and cost-effective for the public. Do I need to remind you of the now-defunct brokerage houses that plowed over their very own clients in the financial meltdown? It is a public fact that Merrill Lynch sold its own bad paper during the 2008 meltdown. It did this by selling all of its shares before its clients, thus driving the unit prices down. Only then did it tell its clients to get out after everything crashed. Despicable!

Some of the biggest financial companies are nothing more than mega-marketing machines that put out these products, which are sold before you catch on to the details. Bottom line, they love VAs because they make a lot of money in the fog of complexity. Each year, no matter what the market does, they get these high fees even if you don't gain high returns. Why should they care?

I believe most of the advisors who sell variable annuities are often not fully aware themselves of the expenses and costs they are passing on to people every day. Once, I had a competing advisor in my office who challenged my analysis, only to sit there embarrassed as I unraveled the many layers of fees and charges. He was a very nice guy, actually, and I felt kind of bad for him. He genuinely wanted to do what was right for his clients but clearly hadn't dug down far enough on the products he used; I knew he just drank the Kool-Aid that his sales managers made him drink.

Summary of Variable Annuity Annual Charges
Based on the Preceding Examples:

(Note: these costs are hypothetical based on averages we have routinely observed over twenty years in practice. Your VA may have lower or higher annual costs.)

M&E 1.25 %
Fund Costs 2.00 %
Turnover   0.75 % (low example here)
Running Total = 4.00 % per year!

However, if you add an income rider that would be another 1.5 percent per year, bringing your total annual costs to a whopping 5.5 percent! Yikes!!

These costs are primarily why so many variable annuity owners watch account values tread water year after year instead of benefiting from the cyclical bull runs in the market. Think about it. How can an investment get anywhere when facing a 4 percent annual headwind of resistance? In other words, if your costs are 4 percent, you need to make 4 percent before you even break even.

There Is Literally No Legitimate Argument for Ownership of the VARIABLE Forms of LIFE INSURANCE or ANNUITIES

All of the supposed reasons an advisor will put a pretty dress on a variable product recommendation, such as perceived benefits, can be achieved with existing alternatives. Such alternatives are more efficient, and do not include the market risk inherent in variable life insurance or variable annuity products.

LIFETIME INCOME RIDERS
AND INCOME PAYOUT OPTIONS

Are lifetime income riders just like a pension from an employer?

A pension for a retiree from a company is derived from an annuity issued by a life insurance company. Many people do not realize when they have a pension, they really have an annuity. They don't pick the company or anything else beside the payout options. They are just glad to have it. Pensions are insured by the Pension Benefit Guaranty Corporation (PBGC). In a pension, you elect a settlement and then no longer have access to the principal and cannot change the terms.

When you buy your own private annuity in the open market to be used as a future pension, you aren't relinquishing ownership and access to the principal. More often than not, you can find higher payouts than employer-sponsored pensions, as well as some additional bells and whistles, such as accelerated benefits for significant health events, extended benefits, and more.

Actually, where is my money in a VA or FIA?

In a *variable annuity*, your money is not part of the insurance company's general account. Your money is invested in mutual fund clones, technically called sub-accounts. In VAs there is no guarantee of your principal by any entity. If you have an income rider attached, it will encumber the insurance company to pay you out via the conditions of the contract.

In a *fixed or fixed index annuity*, your money becomes part of the issuing insurance company's general account. Your funds are not invested in the market. As stated earlier, fixed and fixed index annuities (FIAs) are guaranteed insurance contracts (GICs). These companies are limited to minimal leverage of deposits and many companies have reinsurance agreements with other life insurance companies.

A FINAL WORD ABOUT ANNUITIES

In closing, I do not feel fixed or fixed indexed annuities are automatically for everyone. Many people can benefit from them, but there are always exceptions where they aren't totally necessary. There are appropriate annuities and inappropriate annuities. Furthermore, there are good financial advisors and poor financial advisors. Unfortunately, sometimes advisors recommend annuities that are less than suitable for a client. My overall advice is to approach annuities, like any financial vehicle, with caution, and make sure you fully understand the terms, costs, and conditions before buying.

Chapter 9

FINDING THE RIGHT ADVISOR

The advisor you had during the accumulation stage may not
be the best advisor for the distribution-preservation stage.
The skill sets for the two phases are very different.
~Jeff Cirino, MBA, CFP®, ChFC, CLU, EA

HOW TO BE CERTAIN YOU FIND
AND HIRE THE BEST ADVISOR
FOR YOUR UNIQUE FINANCIAL SITUATION

D on't go it alone.

The rules of the retirement planning game are changing rapidly every day. How do you navigate this? To start, you need a trusted professional with a team who has the skills to solve many types of financial and legal problems. These trusted professionals will not typically be found in the form of your favorite bank teller, nor at the local coffee shop, beauty salon, or golf course. The most complete review available will be with a specialized team of professionals, consisting of a qualified estate

planning attorney, a CPA or Tax Enrolled Agent, and a CFP®
professional, which is a Certified Financial Planner™
professional, someone who is skilled in asset protection,
retirement income planning, and much more.

Watch out for commission brokers

Do you really know how your advisor is being compensated for
the advice he or she is giving you? Furthermore, do you think
you have paid an amount equal to the level of service and value
you have received? Translation: Is the fee you are paying worth
the advice your advisor offers?

No matter where you park your money in the world of financial
risk, it will cost you. You can lower your fees by minimizing
risk. However, if you want to lower fees on your risked money,
then it is critical for you to know what you are currently paying,
so you have a baseline of comparison.

Beware of online "resources"

Today, it is not uncommon for anyone—including retirees—to
jump online to do research. But information online should be
viewed with a very skeptical eye.

One critical question to ask: Are you getting information from a
credible source? This can be very difficult to decipher online.
Information overload is another problem. If you enter the
keyword "revocable trust" on Google, you will be able to access
about 962,000 articles, websites, and "resources" to consider.
Yes, you need to do research, but on the right things, and you
need to know what should be ignored by finding the right help.

Focus your due diligence on finding the right planning team to assist you.

Demand proof!

There's nothing worse than getting sold a bad idea. Slick talk can be very persuasive, but it may prove financially disastrous. When seeking professional advice, we recommend you assess just how accomplished your potential advisor really is. How that person answers the following questions should give you a good idea of their qualifications and passion for their work:

Do You Invest in Your Professional Knowledge?

This question is a great way to gauge the prospective advisor's commitment to staying current on new laws, tax code changes, product innovations, and cutting-edge strategies to help preserve and grow your wealth. If you have a large IRA you're considering moving, for example, you might be swayed by knowing if an advisor participates in regular training around the country alongside an elite group of the nation's top financial professionals, staying abreast of the most tax-efficient strategies for your particular retirement account.

Beware of "financial professionals" who simply pass an exam to become licensed yet never commit to ongoing education beyond that point. Financial advising is an ever-evolving industry, and it may be wise to question the long-term discipline of an advisor who won't commit to staying at the head of his or her class.

Where Do I Start Looking for an Advisor?

One of the best ways to draw from a quality pool of potential advisors is to interview, exclusively, Certified Financial Planners™. Keep in mind, every CFP® professional is not guaranteed to be a 100 percent right fit for you. Even amongst CFP® professionals, advice can and does vary greatly, so you still have to do your own due diligence. But, being board-certified ensures there have been no legal or ethical violations levied on the person who is licensed as a CFP®.

As a CFP® professional, one has to go through the education, background check, degree requirement, financial exams, continuing education, and of course, pass the two-day exam. The exam covers all investments, tax code mastery, estate planning, economics, insurance, and individual retirement planning mastery.

You see, there really is no single license to qualify a financial professional per se. Most new professionals start with a life and annuity license, and they can actually hold themselves out as a financial planner. If one is insurance-only licensed, it is illegal for them to discuss or advise in any way on securities, but a lay person may not realize this distinction.

An advisor with an insurance license and/or a securities license has only the state and their broker dealer as a reporting entity, which limits recourse for the client if they wish to file a complaint.

A CFP® who is also a fee-based financial advisor offers three layers of oversight for the protection of clients:

1. For securities, a fee-based advisor is bound by the state of domicile's Securities Division or the SEC if they manage over $100 million. *The absence of commissions eliminates potential conflicts of interest.*

2. Registered investment advisory firms (or RIAs) are held to the higher "fiduciary" level of responsibility for clients as opposed to commissioned brokers.

A fiduciary is one who will be held to the standard of "always do what's best for the client."

3. A CFP® must answer to the CFP Board of Standards. A CFP® professional can only keep the letters of CFP® as long as there are no ethical or legal violations and there are records of ongoing continuing education.

So, the question comes down to whether or not you want your doctor to be board certified. Many are not. That is a scary thought. Consider that possibility and then ask yourself, "Why would I want to work with a financial advisor who is not board-certified?" Your money is nearly as important as your health.

FINAL THOUGHTS

1. When you are given a formal recommendation, be sure to make them answer in plain language to no less than your complete satisfaction.

2. If you own mutual funds and/or variable annuities, you should have a third-party advisor calculate all of the costs, fees, and charges. Make sure they show you with a third-party source and show you how they arrived at the total costs.

3. Have all your investments "third-partied," meaning the people managing your money and the investment vehicles are separate companies from your financial advisor. Keep your cost of capital low. Costs kill. High costs are not necessary and are quite detrimental to your long-term success.

4. Know the taxability of your investments. A CFP® professional or a CPA can easily explain the tax treatment of your various accounts.

5. Know the difference between risky investments and safer instruments.

6. Make sure you know how much risk you have, especially if you're older than fifty.

7. Demand 100 percent transparency in where and how your money is invested, as well as 100 percent disclosure of an advisor's fee or commission compensation. If they can't answer it and explain it genuinely, then run.

8. In general, avoid variable life insurance and variable annuities, especially in your IRAs. You do not need insurance costs in your IRA.

9. Fixed index annuities should never be confused with variable annuities. They are completely different animals, but

unfortunately, they share the same categorical name: "annuity." That is where the similarities end.

10. Make sure you understand that markets make money; advisors and fund managers can get in the way. Don't fight the efficiency of the markets.

11. Don't let the hyped-up wizards of Wall Street fool you into thinking they are smarter than you. They cannot predict the market or stock moves, either.

12. Stock picking and market timing is inconsistent and more akin to casino gambling than anything else.

13. Don't chase mutual fund track records. A good year or two only means that asset class just happened to do well. When you chase returns, you get burned, plain and simple.

14. Don't allow advisors or salespeople to pressure or rush you. An intelligent, prudent advisor will work at your pace in your plan development.

15. Don't work with insurance-only professionals for your total planning needs. They are missing a whole other world of expertise, and advice will be one-sided.

16. Diversity is the only "free lunch" in finance. With optimal diversity, you normally have greater upside and lesser downside over time.

~Jeff Cirino 2019

ABOUT THE AUTHOR

J eff Cirino, founder and CEO of Alpha Planning, is a well-known fiduciary advisor who has been in practice for more than twenty-five years.

In addition to giving year-round workshops covering topics such as Social Security, tax planning, and investments, Jeff is frequently on radio stations WTAM 1100 and WHK 1420 in Cleveland-Akron, Ohio. Since founding the firm, he has developed his team's skills in using advanced planning concepts, primarily focusing on clients who are nearing or already in retirement.

Jeff has great passion for the challenge of helping usher people through the complex process of the retirement transition. He understands the confusion and stress people may sometimes feel when approaching financial issues at this important phase of their lives.

Throughout the years of growth at his firm, he has written three books prior to *Retirement 2020*: *The Complete Guide to College Funding* (2003), *The Skinny on How to Have a Fat Retirement* (2013), and *The BIG Squeeze: How Boomers Can Survive and Thrive in the New Retirement Frontier.*

Jeff has achieved and maintained through continuing education the following academic and professional designations:

- Executive Master of Business from Baldwin-Wallace university (EMBA)
- Certified Financial Planner™ (CFP®)
- Enrolled Agent, registered with the IRS and qualified to advise, prepare, and represent all matters of taxation before the IRS on the behalf of clients (EA)
- Chartered Financial Consultant® (ChFC®)
- Chartered Life Underwriter® (CLU®)

Although Jeff and his team have a lot of technical knowledge, he is very focused on explaining complex financial concepts in plain English. Jeff feels there is too much avoidable confusion in the industry, and he truly is always looking for ways to make important things understandable for the "everyman" or "everywoman."

Jeff is a lifelong accomplished pianist and guitarist. He lives in Brecksville with his wife, Elizabeth, and sons, Reese and Foster. The family is very active as volunteers for several charities as well as the Cuyahoga Valley National Park.

CONTACT US

I hope you can appreciate my passion and fire for my profession. Also, I hope you recognize my sincere desire to uncover financial deception. Don't let the Wall Street bullies make you think they know something you can't know. They are dead wrong. Not everyone will agree with my assessments, and that is fine. Differing views always exist, but that is what makes America and free enterprise so great.

I wish you all a long, healthy, and prosperous life.

If you'd like to discuss the alternatives to Wall Street's way of doing business that I've outlined in this book, contact our office:

https://alphaplanners.com
Phone: 440.519.0300 | Fax: 440.519.0331
info@alphaplanners.com

Headquarters
6325 Cochran Road, Suite 5
Solon, OH 44139

Independence Office
4807 Rockside Road, Suite 400
Independence, OH 44131

Made in the USA
Middletown, DE
18 April 2021

37877238R00060